A CHURCH
USING ITS SUNDAY SCHOOL

A CHURCH

Using Its Sunday School

J. N. BARNETTE

Convention Press

Nashville, Tennessee

ABOUT THE AUTHOR

JASPER NEWTON BARNETTE was born in Bakersville, Mitchell County, North Carolina, October 3, 1887. His parents were J. D. and Sarah (Jones) Barnette. He was converted in 1900 and baptized into the fellowship of Double Springs Baptist Church, Cleveland County, North Carolina.

He was educated in the public schools of North Carolina. He is a graduate of Shenandoah College and Conservatory, Dayton, Virginia. In 1952 Hardin-Simmons University conferred upon him the honorary degree of L.H.D. (Doctor of Humanity).

Mr. Barnette served as Sunday school superintendent of the Double Springs church with such success that, in 1921, he was called to become associate Sunday school secretary for North Carolina, where he served six years. In 1927 he came to the Sunday School Board as an associate in the Department of Sunday School Administration. In 1943 he became secretary of the newly organized Sunday School Department, in which capacity he served until his retirement in December, 1957.

Dr. Barnette's contribution to the development of the Sunday school movement has been immeasurable. His influence has reached throughout the Southern Baptist Convention territory and into our mission fields. In 1954 Dr. Barnette toured South America in the interest of Bible teaching and Sunday school work. He served as editor of *The Sunday School Builder* from 1943 until 1957. He is author of books whose total circulation in 1957 had reached one million: A CHURCH USING ITS SUNDAY SCHOOL, *The Place of the Sunday School in Evangelism, The Pull of the People, One to Eight,* and *Associational Sunday School Work.*

On March 14, 1912, Mr. Barnette married Edna V. Hawkins of Shelby, North Carolina. They have two children; J. N. Barnette, Jr., and Mary Sue (Barnette) Gulbenk.

CONTENTS

The Sunday School Training Course

THE Sunday School Training Course prepared by the Sunday School Department of the Baptist Sunday School Board is one of the major means of promoting Sunday school work. Its influence is limited only by its use.

The six sections of the course include studies in Bible, doctrines, evangelism, Sunday school leadership and administration, teaching, age group studies, and special studies. The range of the course is broad, for the field of Sunday school work is broad and requires comprehensive and specific training. Sixteen books are required for the completion of each of the three diplomas offered.

The study of the training course is not to be limited to the present Sunday school workers. Most churches need twice as many workers as are now enlisted. This need can be supplied by training additional workers now. Members of the Young People's and Adult classes and older Intermediates should be led to study these books, for thereby will their service be assured. Parents will find help as they study what the Sunday school is trying to do.

Special Note to Instructor:

During your teaching of this book will you check with the Sunday school superintendent and see whether an accurate record of training for the workers is kept. If not, please urge him to set up such a file with an associate superintendent of training in charge. Filing materials—cards, envelopes, or loose-leaf sheets—may be ordered at nominal cost from your nearest Baptist Book Store.

A. V. WASHBURN

Secretary, Sunday School Department
Baptist Sunday School Board

SOME PROJECTED VISUAL
MATERIALS

For Use in Teaching This Book

SEVERAL motion pictures and filmstrips correlate with the material in this book.

You may use the motion picture, *My Church* (10 min.), as a lead into the discussion of chapters 1 and 2.

The filmstrip, *Laws of Sunday School Growth*, may be used to summarize chapter 2, or it may be shown in connection with chapters 5 and 6.

Either the motion picture, *And Make Disciples* (15 min.), or the corresponding filmstrip, *Ye Are Witnesses*, may be used with chapters 3 and 4.

The filmstrip, *An Adequate Training Program*, may be used with chapters 5 and 6, or with chapter 7. The filmstrip, *The Weekly Officers and Teachers' Meeting*, may be used with chapter 7.

Along with the study of chapters 8 and 9 one or both of the following filmstrips may be used:

Class Officers at Work—This is a general treatment, designed to introduce the series of five filmstrips. If you use the first one in the series in connection with chapter 8, it will be well to use the other four in a class officers' clinic, as soon after the training school as possible.

The Christian Teacher—In connection with chapter 9 you may wish to show this filmstrip. You will no doubt wish to use the entire *Teacher Improvement Series* (five filmstrips) at later dates.

FOREWORD

THIS BOOK was born from the desire specifically: (1) to show
churches something of the possibilities of using the Sunday
school in the work of a church, and (2) to help the leaders
understand how to use the Sunday school. All of the Sunday
schools will find the study well suited to their programs. The
Sunday schools conducted by classes will see the advantages
of the department pattern of organization as such schools
respond to the challenge to "move up." The book has in its
various revisions reflected the increasing need for departments in all schools.

While there is no mention of the minister of education, his
importance is not overlooked. In many churches the minister
of education is the superintendent of the Sunday school. In
all situations he will team with the pastor in working through
the elected Sunday school officers and teachers as together
they lead the church to use its Sunday school to carry out the
commission of Christ.

Chapter 1

The Possibilities of a Sunday School in the Work of a Church

I. THE CHURCH AND ITS MISSION

1. *Established and Commissioned by Jesus*

The agencies for bringing in the kingdom of God are the churches.

Jesus established the church and gave it the task of representing him on earth. Jesus was very specific in what he wanted a church to do in the world. During the forty days from his resurrection to his ascension, it seemed that the burden of his heart was to get his followers to understand their mission in the world. In Matthew 28:19–20, he states definitely that they were to go into all the world and make disciples for him, baptize them, then teach them to observe all the things which he had commanded. Evidently this means evangelism in its fullest sense and not occasional revival meetings alone. In Acts 1:8 Jesus tells his followers to go into Jerusalem, then Judea, then Samaria, and then on to the uttermost parts of the earth. Theirs was to be an aggressive, continuous, ever-widening task. Salvation is a personal matter and each generation must be evangelized. The followers of Jesus in each generation should do their best to give the gospel of Christ to every creature on this earth. The Great Commission teaches that every Christian should go to the limit of his ability and make disciples for Christ Jesus and then teach them to go and make other disciples. This is the method of Jesus and is his method for each succeeding generation of Christians until he comes again.

2. *Empowered and Directed by Jesus*

Jesus promised to be with his disciples in the work of advancing his kingdom. He told them that all power in heaven

1

and on earth is available for his children in the work of making disciples. He gave his word that he would be with them all the days, no matter what kind of days, in their efforts to make disciples for him. All power in heaven and on earth was available for Peter and Paul; and like power in all fulness is available for Christians today, as long as they strive to witness for Christ, teach his Word, and preach his gospel. The purpose of their enduement with spiritual power was to advance the kingdom of God. In the fifteenth and sixteenth chapters of John, Jesus tells his disciples that he will send the Holy Spirit who will guide them. Jesus established the church, Jesus commissioned the church, Jesus empowered the church, and Jesus directs the church. The church is the agency of Jesus in the world for the propagation of his kingdom.

3. *Methods of Making Disciples Given by Jesus*

Jesus told his followers just how they were to make disciples for him. They were to do three things—witness, preach, and teach. The early disciples made use of all three of these methods.

(1) *Every disciple should witness*

Jesus told the disciples to let their light shine. Several times it is recorded that Paul related the account of his conversion. From the study of Paul's work in the book of Acts, it is evident that he never tired of telling of his Damascus road experience. No doubt this experience was related over and over during the months spent in Corinth, Ephesus, Rome, and other places. When Paul needed a strong appeal, he told his experience. The blind man when pressed for an answer replied: "One thing I know, that, whereas I was blind, now I see" (John 9:25).

Much of the present-day preaching and teaching consists in telling others what to do rather than in telling of what Christ has done. Honest and sincere witnessing is effective. A living witness is an effective witness of the reality, power, and goodness of God. Paul said to the Corinthian Christians that they were known and read of all men. Sunday school pupils may not remember many things the officers and teachers say, but they can never get away from the silent influence of what they are.

(2) *Preaching is to be magnified*

Preaching had a prominent place in the work of Jesus. The early disciples made use of preaching. Paul was a great preacher. Paul said, "I am appointed a preacher" (2 Tim. 1:11). He said to Timothy, "Preach the word." Preaching has been one of the major methods for advancing the kingdom of God. Sunday school officers and teachers need to evaluate preaching as one of the major methods of ministering to the spiritual needs of people. Preachers should heed the admonition Paul gave to Timothy—"Preach the word." The gospel was the power of God unto salvation two thousand years ago. The gospel is the power of God unto salvation today. The preacher's only message to lost people is Jesus. Thank God for the preacher and for gospel preaching!

(3) *Teaching is necessary*

Jesus was called a teacher. He taught his disciples. He put teaching in the Great Commission. Paul made great use of teaching. He stayed at Corinth a year and six months "teaching the word of God among them" (Acts 18:11). He stayed at Ephesus two years and used the school of Tyrannus (Acts 19:9). He dwelt two years in his own hired house at Rome "preaching the kingdom of God, and teaching those things which concern the Lord Jesus Christ" (Acts 28:30–31). In 2 Timothy 2:2 he states, "The things that thou hast heard of me . . . the same commit thou to faithful men, who shall be able to teach others also."

Teaching is an important part of the work of evangelism. Christianity almost passed from the earth when the teaching function of the churches was neglected. Christianity has made rapid progress during the past 125 years since the teaching function of the churches has been revived and used. Christianity produced the Sunday school.

The present-day preaching and teaching should stress the imparting of Bible truth along with the exhorting and warning. Teaching is also an important part of enlistment. The "teaching them to observe all things whatsoever I have commanded" part of the Great Commission should receive more attention.

4. *Churches Primal in the Program of Jesus*

The kingdom of God prospers most in communities where there are churches. Churches are essential to the progress of the kingdom of God. Jesus came to "seek and to save that which was lost." His method of reaching people with the message of salvation is through churches. It is of the utmost importance that the followers of Christ establish churches in every community.

Every kind of mission work must wait upon the churches. The money necessary for the promotion of the work must come from the churches. The workers must come from the churches. The authority for the establishment of agencies and the propagation of plans must come from the churches. The way to strengthen the mission work is to build New Testament churches in every community. When there are enough strong, active, sacrificing, working, giving churches, every phase of Christian work will be strengthened.

Since the churches are the agencies for bringing in the kingdom of God, Christian people should serve earnestly to build a strong church in every community. Not only should there be churches that are strong numerically and financially, but strong spiritually, mighty bulwarks of spiritual power.

We come now to study the possibilities of a Sunday school in the work of a church.

Let us pray that the Eternal Father of our Lord Jesus Christ, who gave us the church and its task, shall help us all—pastors, deacons, Sunday school workers, and all Christian leaders—to see the possibilities of the church agency known as the Sunday school.

II. THE POSSIBILITIES OF A SUNDAY SCHOOL IN THE WORK OF A CHURCH

1. *Value Recognized by Baptist Leaders*

In 1902 Dr. E. Y. Mullins said: "The Sunday school must more and more prove a factor of power in the pastor's work. Already in many churches the Sunday school is the chief and almost only hope for church growth. But whether in the family church, or the church among the masses of the great city, or the country church, the Sunday school will remain the most hopeful field of evangelistic endeavor. If the writer may be permitted to bear witness to a personal experience, he would say that, all things considered, the most fruitful year in fifteen of his pastoral effort was most intimately connected with the Sunday school."

In 1911 Dr. J. M. Frost said: "Everything the church holds dear, every great interest and enterprise in which the church is engaged, everything which the church needs, whether for making it strong and mighty within, or powerful and projective in its influence upon the community—all is fostered and magnified in this school of the church, first made possible and then brought to pass.

"The school becomes as an agency what the church makes it; is capable of almost indefinite expansion in church efficiency as a channel for the output of its energy and life. While holding stedfastly to the one basal purpose of teaching the Scriptures, the Sunday school has yet greatly widened in its aim. As a force for study and teaching the Word of God; as a force for evangelizing and bringing lost sinners to the Saviour; as a force for instruction and education in the mightiest things claiming the attention of men; as a force for mission operation in the worldwide sense; as a force for making Christian character in men and women; and for opening the door of usefulness on a large scale—in all these things so essential in the life and mission of the church, the Sunday school holds rank among its very first and chosen agencies."

In 1930 Arthur Flake said: "The Sunday school presents an

unparalleled opportunity for the successful promotion of practically every phase of church activity as well as the utilization of every member of the church and congregation in useful service without detracting from the effectiveness of the Sunday school as a Bible teaching agency, or interfering in the least degree with the work of any other desirable and useful church agency."

2. Suited for Present Conditions

(1) Complex conditions exist

In the immediate past lost people went to church services because of social contacts. In small towns and in country communities the church services offered the major means of community gatherings. Now almost multitudinous attractions lure people away from the churches. Sunday athletics, Sunday radio programs, good roads and automobiles, an abundance of magazines, and Sunday newspapers show the trend. These attractions are prevalent in every type of community. In many communities Sunday evening has become a special time for friends to entertain friends. No longer can a congregation be assembled by ringing a church bell. The automobile horns, the radios in almost every home, talking pictures with their sound features drown out the church bells. Worldly attractions allure the multitudes. Complex conditions multiply the difficulties in reaching people for any kind of a church service.

(2) Personal efforts are necessary

It requires personal work to reach people for church services today. The natural inclination of people is away from churches. People are not seeking churches, churches must seek people. In the fifteenth chapter of Luke, Jesus pictures the good shepherd going out seeking one individual lost sheep. The work was definite. That is the method necessary for present conditions.

The Sunday school as a church agency is well suited for the present complex conditions. It modestly claims the whole range of human life for its field. Its organization embodies small classes with close grading, thus definitely locating personal responsibility for each individual. It has some of the most capable church members as officers and teachers. It has numbers as one of the four major objectives. It has personal and regular visitation as a major method of reaching the masses. It has the strong appeal of regular Bible study in closely graded groups. It has Bible evangelism as its aim. It has preaching attendance as one of the goals for each officer, teacher, and pupil. It has a record system that gives a complete record of each individual enrolled. It has an organization large enough to take a religious census for the purpose of locating all prospects. Thus, in its objectives, methods, and organization the Sunday school fixes individual responsibility for locating, reaching, teaching, and winning every available person.

3. *Guarantees That the Bible Will Be Taught*
(1) *God the Father makes Bible teaching imperative*

There are some imperative statements in the Old Testament relative to studying the Scriptures:

"And these words, which I command thee this day, shall be in thine heart: and thou shalt teach them diligently unto thy children, and shalt talk of them when thou sittest in thine house, and when thou walkest by the way, and when thou liest down, and when thou risest up. And thou shalt bind them for a sign upon thine hand, and they shall be as frontlets between thine eyes. And thou shalt write them upon the posts of thy house, and on thy gates" (Deut. 6:6-9).

"Gather the people together, . . . that they may hear, and that they may learn, and fear the Lord your God, and observe to do all the words of this law: and that their children, which have not known any thing, may hear, and learn to fear the Lord your God, as long as ye live in the land whither ye go over Jordan to possess it" (Deut. 31:12-13).

These emphatic words indicate the importance that God the Father places upon the study of the Scriptures.

(2) *Jesus the Son and Saviour commands Bible teaching in the Great Commission*

When Jesus gave his disciples the Commission, "teach them to observe all things whatsoever I have commanded," it is evident that he had in mind the teaching of the word of God as preserved and handed down to man in the Bible. The Great Commission as given in Matthew 28:19–20 seems to be a summing up of what Jesus would have his followers to do in the world. Teaching the Bible is made imperative by the commands of the Lord.

It is clear that a church ought to teach the Bible all of the time to every available individual. Bible study is essential in all Christian work. It is essential in making disciples; in informing disciples; in the growth of disciples; and for Christian workers as they go making other disciples.

(3) *A properly functioning Sunday school in a church guarantees that the Bible will be taught*

A church's most effective means of teaching the Bible is through a properly functioning Sunday school. The Sunday school has the Bible as its one and only textbook. The Sunday school meets every Sunday. It provides Bible study for all, beginning with the little child and continuing through the years to the oldest adult. It has graded pupils, graded buildings, graded lessons, and graded activities. A properly functioning Sunday school guarantees that the Bible will be taught to all ages all of the time.

Because a church has a Sunday school in name only does not guarantee that the Bible will be taught. It is one thing for a church to have a Sunday school and another thing for a church to use it. However, if a Sunday school is made to function properly, it makes possible regular Bible study.

4. Can Be Used as the Chief Agency in Doing the Chief Work of a Church

(1) *Evangelism is the chief work of a church*

Christ's mission in the world was to seek and to save the lost. He allowed nothing to turn him from it. His last command teaches us that the chief work of his followers is to make disciples for him.

Evangelism is the chief work of a church. Evangelism should have the first place in the program of every organization within a church. A church that allows anything else to be first will find that it has been switched to a sidetrack. Churches find themselves surrounded with all kinds of opportunities to minister to people in the name of Christ, and the temptations to turn aside from the main task of the churches are many. The purpose of the whole Bible is the redemption of lost man through the blood of Jesus. "Christ came into the world to save sinners, of whom I am chief" is the very heart of the gospel. Evangelism is the chief asset of a church.

(2) *The Sunday school is the chief agency of a church in evangelism*

A Sunday school provides a church with its greatest field for evangelism. The Sunday school puts major emphasis upon reaching people—all classes of people—the lost as well as the saved. Churches have found it possible through an adequate Sunday school organization to reach nearly all of the available Junior and Intermediate boys and girls. It is also possible to reach large numbers of Young People and Adults who are not Christians.

The Sunday school has the Bible as its only textbook. It teaches the Bible Sunday after Sunday to large numbers of lost people. The Sunday school, as a church organization, has as one of its primary tasks the teaching of the Bible to lost people. Because the Sunday school immediately precedes the preaching service, it is easy to lead the lost in Sunday school to remain for the preaching service, and thus provide a perennial evangelistic opportunity.

A Sunday school provides a church with its greatest force for evangelism. In reaching the lost, in teaching the Bible, in putting the lost into the preaching service, in doing personal work, the Sunday school officers and teachers constitute a force that is regular and resultful.

5. *Makes Possible Full-time Work in Every Church*

Many churches do not have preaching every Sunday. It has become customary to call this group of churches "part-time churches," meaning that they do not have preaching every Sunday. They are not necessarily part-time churches. Most of them have Sunday schools, and thus have a service every Sunday. The task of the pastor with two or more churches is to plan for and lead these churches to do full-time work even though he cannot be present every Sunday. A properly functioning Sunday school makes possible full-time work in every church. In the smaller churches, with preaching only one Sunday in the month, there will be time on the three remaining Sundays for more Bible study, with ample time for good opening and closing programs. The pastor with two or more churches can use the Sunday schools to promote Bible study, worship, evangelism, training, and giving. He can also use the Sunday school in giving out information regarding every phase of denominational life and in furnishing a place of service for the church members. All of this work can be carried on all of the time even though the pastor cannot be present every Sunday.

A pastor with two or more churches will find in the weekly meeting of the Sunday school officers and teachers an effective means for promoting the work of each church. Many of the capable workers of a church are in the Sunday school organization, or should be. A weekly meeting of these workers gives a wonderful opportunity to inform, inspirit, and direct them in the four-fold task of reaching, teaching, winning, and developing people for Christ.

A pastor with as many as four churches can attend at least one such meeting in each church every month; and in most instances, he can attend two and sometimes more. He should see that these meetings are planned so that he can attend whenever it is possible for him to do so. The meetings should be held each week even though the pastor cannot attend every week.

In addition to using the Sunday school, a church with part-time preaching will find a Baptist Training Union most helpful. Any church can have a good Baptist Training Union meeting every Sunday evening with a place for all of the church members to study how to be stronger and more useful Christians. The only thing necessary is for the pastor to see that the churches are organized for this work, making sure that capable leaders are in charge, and then guide, direct, and encourage the work.

QUESTIONS FOR REVIEW

1. Write a brief paragraph on the title of this book.
2. What is the mission of a church as given in Matthew 28:19–20?
3. Discuss the place of churches in the promotion of the kingdom of God.
4. Why is the Sunday school suited for present conditions?
5. How does the Sunday school make possible full-time work in every church?

OUTLINE

I. THE CHURCH AND ITS MISSION

1. Established and Commissioned by Jesus
2. Empowered and Directed by Jesus
3. Methods of Making Disciples Given by Jesus
4. Churches Primal in the Program of Jesus

II. THE POSSIBILITIES OF A SUNDAY SCHOOL IN THE WORK OF A CHURCH

1. Value Recognized by Baptist Leaders
2. Suited for Present Conditions
3. Guarantees That the Bible Will Be Taught
4. Can Be used as the Chief Agency in Doing the Chief Work of a Church
5. Makes Possible Full-time Work in Every Church

Chapter 2

The Sunday School Reaching People

BECAUSE OF what is involved—Bible study, soul-winning, Christian growth, Christian service—the work of reaching people is a major task for a church. Because of the opportunities offered by the presence of large numbers in the church services, the task of reaching people is an imperative obligation upon church leaders.

I. TEACHINGS OF THE BIBLE ABOUT REACHING PEOPLE

1. *God's Desire for Numbers*

In Deuteronomy 31:11–12, the words of God the Father teach plainly and emphatically that the people, all the people—all ages and all classes—should be gathered together for Bible study: "When all Israel is come to appear before the Lord thy God in the place which he shall choose, thou shalt read this law before all Israel in their hearing. Gather the people together, men, and women, and children, and thy stranger that is within thy gates, that they may hear, and that they may learn, and fear the Lord your God, and observe to do all the words of this law." The blessings and promises of heaven are not for the favored only, but even the strangers are included if they will come and accept the promises of God.

In John 3:16, Jesus, who came from God, tells us that God loved the world including the whole human race: "For God so loved the world, that he gave his only begotten Son, that whosoever believeth in him should not perish, but have everlasting life."

The story of the prodigal son is a plain word picture of the love of God for all people. Jesus here shows to the world the Father heart of God. God loved the wayward son in the depths of sin and God loved the rebellious son in the home.

Again in Matthew 18:14, the word is "Even so it is not the will of your Father which is in heaven, that one of these little ones should perish."

These passages forever magnify, dignify, and glorify soul-winning. If God, the creator of all things, yearns after the souls of all men, then what a privilege it is to be an instrument in his all-powerful hands to go even into the highways and hedges and tell sinning men, women, boys, and girls of the love of God.

2. Jesus' Ministry to Numbers

The coming of Jesus into the world is proof of his love for the lost multitudes. "For the Son of man is come to seek and to save that which was lost" (Luke 19:10). "But God commendeth his love toward us, in that, while we were yet sinners, Christ died for us" (Rom. 5:8). ". . . for I am not come to call the righteous, but sinners to repentance" (Matt. 9:13).

In Luke 15:1–10, Jesus shows to what extreme a church should go in seeking the people for Bible study. As long as there is one person on the outside, the spirit manifested in these parables should be the spirit of the followers of Christ.

These and many other passages vividly portray to the world something of the wonder of the love of God in Christ Jesus for the lost.

3. Churches Commanded to Go After Numbers

"Go ye therefore, and teach all nations, baptizing them in the name of the Father, and of the Son, and of the Holy Ghost: teaching them to observe all things whatsoever I have commanded you: and, lo, I am with you alway, even unto the end of the world" (Matt. 28:19–20). "Then said Jesus to them again, Peace be unto you: as my Father hath sent me, even so send I you" (John 20:21). "And the lord said unto the servant, Go out into the highways and hedges, and compel them to come in, that my house may be filled" (Luke 14:23).

The attitude of a church in reaching people for Bible study is not an optional matter. The task of reaching people is made imperative by the Word of God, by the example of Jesus, by the parables of Jesus, and by the commands of Jesus.

II. BIBLE CONCEPTION OF REACHING PEOPLE ESSENTIAL

1. A Vision of the Unreached Multitudes Needed

In Matthew 9:35 we read, "And Jesus went about all the cities and villages, teaching in their synagogues, and preaching the gospel of the kingdom, and healing every sickness and every disease among the people." Then in the thirty-sixth verse we read, "But when he saw the multitudes, he was moved with compassion on them, because they fainted, and were scattered abroad, as sheep having no shepherd." Where were the multitudes? Evidently they were not in the synagogues. According to the words of Jesus himself, they were scattered abroad as sheep not having a shepherd.

Where are the multitudes today? Evidently they are not in the church buildings. In fact, the church buildings would not hold even the church members. Yet, there are millions of people who are not even enrolled in any Sunday school.

Over and over Jesus urged the twelve to lift up their eyes and look on the fields. They saw only their own people, the Jews. Many Sunday school officers and teachers see only the ones enrolled in Sunday school, and some see only the ones in attendance. When Paul saw the multitudes, Jews and Gentiles, he was ready to obey Jesus, regardless of the dangers. A vision of the unreached multitudes and of their lost condition is necessary to move churches out into the highways and hedges.

2. A Compassion for the Lost Essential

When Jesus saw the multitudes, he had compassion. The words, "When Jesus saw the multitudes, he was moved with compassion," do not indicate a casual mood of Jesus nor a sudden or passing emotion. They present the constant attitude and the invariable feeling of Jesus toward people. The compassion of Jesus for the multitudes never lifted from his great heart. Over and over the Bible declares God to be full of compassion. "Like as a father pitieth his children, so the Lord pitieth them that fear him" (Psalm 103:13). The compassion of Jesus is the expression of God's compassion toward men.

No doubt a vision of the lost multitudes would move Christian people today. A lack of compassion on the part of many churches may account in a large measure for the meager results in winning people to Christ. The compassion of Christians should match the commission of Jesus. A positive, strong emphasis must start in the lives of the leaders and then spread throughout the whole church membership. Genuine love for the souls of people is a mighty motive. The seeking note is the winning note. When a church stops seeking, it ceases growing.

3. An Understanding of the Value of a Soul Vital

Jesus placed great value upon the individual—"Ye are of more value than many sparrows" (Luke 12:7). "How much then is a man better than a sheep?" (Matt. 12:12). ". . . joy shall be in heaven over one sinner that repenteth" (Luke 15:7). "And he calleth his own sheep by name, and leadeth them out" (John 10:3).

Jesus used some strong statements in an effort to help man understand the value of a soul. "For what is a man profited, if he shall gain the whole world, and lose his own soul? or what shall a man give in exchange for his soul?" (Matt. 16:26). "And if thy right eye offend thee, pluck it out, and cast it from thee: for it is profitable for thee that one of thy members should perish, and not that thy whole body should be cast into hell" (Matt. 5:29). "And if thy right hand offend thee, cut it off, and cast it from thee; for it is profitable for thee that one of thy members should perish, and not that thy whole body should be cast into hell" (Matt. 5:30).

4. The Obligation of the Churches Unquestionable

"Son of man, I have made thee a watchman unto the house of Israel: therefore hear the word at my mouth, and give them warning from me. When I say unto the wicked, Thou shalt surely die; and thou givest him not warning, nor speakest to warn the wicked from his wicked way, to save his life; the same wicked man shall die in his iniquity; but his blood will I require at thine hand. Yet if thou warn the wicked, and he turn not from his wickedness, nor from his wicked way, he shall die in his iniquity; but thou hast delivered thy soul" (Ezek. 3:17–19). "Go ye therefore, and teach all nations, baptizing them in the name of the Father, and of the Son, and of the Holy Ghost: teaching them to observe all things whatsoever I have commanded you: and, lo, I am with you alway, even unto the end of the world" (Matt. 28:19–20).

Paul could not escape his obligation to preach the gospel (1 Cor. 9:16). He felt and accepted the obligation, not only to minister to his kinsmen in the flesh, but to fulfil his obligation to the Gentiles (Rom. 1:14).

Reaching people is not a question of convenience, but of divine compulsion.

Some churches are deceived as to the importance of reaching people. Such expressions as, It is not numbers that count, but quality, may have some truth, but not all the truth. Sometimes leaders place quality against numbers. The statement, I had rather have a good Sunday school than a big one, comes from a heart that has been deceived by the forces of evil, from a heart of indifference, or from a heart that is seeking to cover failure with pious platitudes. Any impression or suggestion against numbers for Bible study does not come from heaven, because the invitation of heaven is "Whosoever will, let him come." The command of heaven is "Go out into the highways and hedges, and compel them to come in, that my house may be filled" (Luke 14:23).

Hell is against numbers studying the Word of God. The devil is continually doing all he can to block every movement on the part of Christian people to lead the multitudes to study the Bible. The devil is afraid of the Word of God. The Word of God is the sword of the Spirit.

The command of Christ is to go into all the world, and the spirit of Christ is the spirit of compassion.

III. A Church Using Its Sunday School to Reach People

First, let it be said that a church can reach people—large numbers of people. However, people must be sought and won to regular attendance. Churches that wait for the people to come will be disappointed. The scriptural teaching is that churches must go out and compel the people to come in. The first test of a Sunday school is the test of numbers. A church should measure its work in reaching people by the number who ought to be in the Sunday school.

If a church does not have more in regular attendance in its Sunday school than there are resident church members, it is evident that the Sunday school is not as large as it should be or as large as it could be made. All of the resident church members should be enrolled in the Sunday school. Counting the Cradle Roll, Nursery, Beginner, and Primary groups, and those from the Junior age up who are not church members, it is evident that there should be many more in Sunday school than there are resident church members. Many churches are using their Sunday schools to reach people. Churches by the use of the methods presented in this chapter have been successful in meeting the numbers test.

The experience of a large number of churches proves that a church must do regularly five things if its Sunday school reaches people in ever-increasing numbers. It must know the people who ought to be in the Sunday school, secure additional workers, provide adequate space, train the workers, and maintain regular visitation.

1. Knowing Who Ought to Be in the Sunday School

This information can be secured from three sources,—the Sunday school roll, the church roll, the religious census.

(1) Include every person on roll in the Sunday school

Every Sunday school should have an accurate record of each individual enrolled. If such a record is kept, the church will have available definite information about the group of people most easily ministered unto. They may be chronic

absentees, but they are on the roll. They are on the regular
roll, for there is no other for any Sunday school. Because of
their enrolment they have at least some interest in the school,
and the school has an inescapable obligation to them.

(2) *Check the church roll*

It is a serious indictment against Southern Baptists that as
yet approximately 50 per cent of the church members are not
enrolled in Sunday school. A church will usually find a large
list of prospects by checking the church roll against the
Sunday school roll, thus securing the names of all the church
members not enrolled in Sunday school. Individual census
cards should be made out for the church members not enrolled in Sunday school, giving the name, address, and ap-
proximate age.

(3) *Take a religious census*

Every church will find it profitable to take a census at least
once each year, provided that the census is used. It pays to
take a complete census. If the work is not well done, the results will be disappointing. The necessary steps in planning
for and taking a census are simple and can be used by any
church:

>Define all of the territory to be canvassed.

>Arrange the territory by blocks, streets, roads, or sections.

>Enlist personally a sufficient number of census takers.

>Secure the census cards and any other needed supplies. (The
>census cards can be ordered from the Baptist Sunday
>School Board or from the state Baptist Book Store.)

>Set aside a day and an hour for doing the work.

>Instruct the census takers. Those who take the census should:

>Go into every home.

>Use a card for EACH individual.

>Get the information firsthand.

>Fill in every blank on EACH card.

>Get the EXACT AGE of EACH individual.

>See that initials and names are correct.

>Complete the territory assigned.

When the territory is finished, return the information immediately to the church.

The information should be put in proper shape to be used.

The census cards should be sorted. First, take out cards for all those already enrolled in the Sunday school and all those who are in any way prospects for the Sunday school.

Census cards should be made for all those on the Sunday school roll and on the church roll if they were not found in the census. There will then be a census card for each person enrolled in the Sunday school, and one for each prospect, including the resident church members not found in the census.

The next step is to grade all of the cards into seven age groups recommended and used in Southern Baptist Sunday schools:

Birth through three years—Cradle Roll and Nursery

Four and five years—Beginners

Six, seven, and eight years—Primaries

Nine, ten, eleven, and twelve years—Juniors

Thirteen, fourteen, fifteen, and sixteen years—Intermediates

Seventeen through twenty-four years—Young People

Twenty-five years and up—Adults

The various age groups should next be rechecked and any remaining duplication eliminated.

The next step is to divide the cards into classes. As far as possible, enough classes and departments should be set up to take care of all the people, enrolled or not enrolled. As further visitation reveals people who cannot attend, they should be assigned to an Extension department.

There should be four Nursery departments for children under four who attend with some degree of regularity. The unenrolled babies found in the census are assigned to the Cradle Roll. There should be a visitor for every six to eight homes in which there are Cradle Roll babies.

There should be a worker for every five to seven Beginners, and a teacher for every five to seven Primaries. Beginning with the Juniors the sexes should be separated. There should be a class for every six to eight Juniors. A class should be provided for every eight to ten Intermediates. The classes for Young People will vary in size. There should be a class for every ten to twenty possibilities of Young People. There should be a class for about every ten to twenty-five Adults. Some classes for Adults will have fewer than twenty. All classes should be graded on the age basis.

After the arrangement of the cards into class groups, the information is now ready to be tabulated. Five or six copies of each list should be made—one each for the pastor, superintendent, associate superintendent, department superintendent if the Sunday school has departments, teacher, and class officers.

2. Securing Additional Officers and Teachers

If additional classes are started, it will be necessary to enlist additional teachers. The primary problem of a pastor and superintendent in building a Sunday school is to secure and keep an adequate number of the right kind of officers and teachers.

(1) How can we secure additional officers and teachers?

a. Pray for them.—When Jesus saw the multitudes, he commanded his disciples to pray for more laborers. A pastor and superintendent should pray and lead the church to pray for workers. There should be prayer without ceasing in the worship service, in the prayer meeting, in the weekly officers and teachers' meeting, and in the secret places.

b. Preach about the need for workers.—It will help for the pastor to preach occasionally upon the privilege of Christian service; upon the responsibility of Christian people; upon the rewards of Christian service; and upon the need for more workers. Such messages will help the people to see the opportunities, feel the urge, and accept the task.

The superintendent also should talk about the needs from the platform, personally, and upon every opportunity.

c. Select them from the church roll.—The pastor and superintendent should take the church roll and carefully select prospective workers. The prospective workers may not have had experience, but it will pay to select the best available persons and then train them for their work. A permanent list of prospective workers should be kept, and these prospects should be given every available opportunity as supply teachers and officers.

d. Enlist them in definite work.—After a decision has been made to start a class or department, the pastor and superintendent should take the list of prospective workers and prayerfully find the person best suited for the work. The individual should be asked to meet the pastor and superintendent at the church building for a conference. It will be better to go to the church building and thus guarantee that all distractions will be removed. After the task has been discussed, there should be a season of prayer. If the individual is not enlisted, try another person, and thus on and on until a worker has been secured. Workers for the Extension department and the Cradle Roll should be enlisted the same way.

e. Encourage them to be faithful.—The new workers will need encouragement and aid. Certainly the pastor and superintendent will encourage and help the workers to succeed.

If a pastor and superintendent will do these five things and do them seriously, intelligently, and regularly, they will get the needed workers. However, they must realize that it takes time, prayer, and hard work to keep a growing Sunday school supplied with an adequate number of the right kind of workers.

(2) *When should additional officers and teachers be secured?*

Additional officers and teachers should be secured whenever they are needed.

a. Immediately.—Without doubt, the present is the best time to begin! Conditions do not, as a rule, get better by waiting. If the pastor and superintendent will study the present organization, no doubt they will find where additional classes should be started immediately. It is likely that the doing of this work will stimulate renewed interest.

b. Periodically.—The present classes should be studied, and as often as necessary additional classes should be organized to take care of growing situations. It will be necessary to keep on organizing additional classes if the Sunday school is kept growing. Unless new classes are started, the growth will soon cease.

c. At promotion time.—Nearly every Sunday school should organize one or more classes at promotion time. Promoting pupils into classes that are already full or into classes that are not congenial because of a wide difference in ages is disastrous. Whenever there is a need, provision should be made in advance for forming new classes for the pupils who will be promoted. In this way a great and serious leakage will be stopped, and the Sunday school will continue to grow.

3. *Providing Adequate Space*

In most churches the present building can be arranged to take care of more classes or departments and thus provide for the growth of the Sunday school. In many of the one-room buildings additional classes could be started by the use of curtains and screens. Many of the present churches are not using one half of the available space. In one church a class of twenty-five men was occupying a room large enough to accommodate the Junior and Intermediate departments with eight classes in each department.

More space can be provided by the erection of new buildings. Churches should not limit the growth of the Sunday school by waiting because they are not financially able to erect expensive church buildings. Such churches can erect buildings of a type that the members can pay for, and thus make it possible to reach more people.

Care should be taken to see that the members of the building committee know the needs of every department of the church. Too often building committees without any knowledge of a Sunday school and Baptist Training Union have built costly buildings and churches have tried without success to put the Sunday school classes and Training Union into the ill-planned buildings. The Baptist Sunday School

Board, through its Department of Church Architecture, is prepared to furnish information and guidance relative to church buildings.

4. Train the Workers

After the additional workers have been selected and enlisted, they should be trained for the work assigned to them. Not many people are conversant with the right plans and methods of doing Sunday school work. They need to be informed. Teachers will need constant help and guidance in learning what to teach and also in mastering the best methods of teaching.

The pastor and Sunday school superintendent should see that a weekly officers and teachers' meeting is conducted and that frequent training schools are held, making special provision for the new and prospective workers. From week to week the pastor and superintendent may desire to place in the hands of each new worker a piece of helpful literature on some important phase of Sunday school work. A personal conference of the pastor and superintendent with the new workers from time to time will help in guiding the worker in his preparation.

5. Maintain Regular Visitation

Visitation is the chief factor in Sunday school growth. It is the final step in actually reaching people. A Sunday school may have adequate space properly arranged, a sufficient number of classes, excellent teaching, attractive worship programs—and how vital they are; but without visitation all these things will be at least a partial failure.

(1) The basis for visitation is scriptural

The basis for visitation is found in the Bible—portrayed in the example of Jesus, made imperative by the commands of Jesus, magnified by the teachings of Jesus, practiced by the early disciples, and, because of the marvelous results of the early Christians, forever made worthy of adoption and use by Christians everywhere.

The Bible is the authority for visiting, and the lost condition of the multitudes is the incentive. The "compel" in the parable of the great supper, the "importunity" of the friend that unwillingly lends at midnight, the "until he finds" in the story of the lost sheep, the "by her continual coming" in the story of the unjust judge, the "seek diligently until she find it" in the parable of the piece of money—all teach Sunday school workers the secret of the successful visitor and soul-winner.

Human weaknesses and love of ease have led many Christian workers away from the methods of Jesus and the practice of the early disciples.

(2) *The motives for visitation are spiritual*

There must be some inner urge if officers and teachers are to continue steadfastly in the work of visitation. And this urge must be based upon something stronger and higher than the size of the class or the percentage of the class grade.

a. The condition of a lost soul.—The condition of a lost soul brought Christ to this earth. The same motive sent Paul out to suffer hardness as a good soldier of Jesus Christ, drove Carey to India, led Livingstone to Africa, and leads stalwart men and lovely women to live for Christ. Nothing short of a realization of the condition of a lost soul will keep Sunday school officers and teachers going continuously after people.

b. The value of a life.—Jesus placed an inestimable value upon life, one life. "What will a man give in exchange for his soul?" As far as is known, the ability of the human will is unlimited; the capacity of the memory is boundless; the imagination is stopped only by the reaches of the universe; the depth, breadth, and height of the human heart for love and sympathy has no limitations; the spiritual growth of the soul finds completeness only in him who is the one altogether lovely. Only heavenly mathematics can measure the influence of a life. Guiding, shaping, and enlisting these limitless powers, capacities, and influences for Christ is the work of Sunday school officers and teachers—and what glorious work it is! Such a conception of a life will at once lift visitation out of the realm of drudgery and make it a blessed privilege.

c. The privilege of serving Jesus.—Mary Magdalene, Joanna, and Susanna ministered to Jesus in person. How can Christians today minister to Jesus? He says, "Inasmuch as ye have done it unto one of the least . . . ye have done it unto me" (Matt. 25:40).

(3) *The benefits of visitation are sure*

Personal, Christlike visitation brings many rich blessings that cannot be had in any other way or from any other source.

a. Visitation provides the teacher with valuable information.—Visitation brings the workers in intimate contact with the needs of the pupils. The needs of people provide a strong incentive. A real human need pulls at the heart of a Christian. Personal contact with some member of the class who is in trouble or distress gives an added depth, warmth, sympathy, and passion to one's teaching.

A reasonable amount of time spent in intelligent visiting will aid greatly in preparing the teacher in mind and spirit for the important work of guiding the members of the class in real Bible study on Sunday morning.

b. Visitation will win for the teacher the respect, love, and confidence of the pupil.—Without the respect, love, and confidence of the pupil the teacher's work will be as sounding brass and tinkling cymbals. The teaching will be more effective if regular, intelligent visitation is carried on.

Warmhearted, passion-driven teachers and class officers will usually have warm hearted, interested people with whom to work. If the welfare of the individual is the main purpose of the officers and teachers, then those in greatest need will be the ones receiving the most tender and prayerful attention. Such interest is bound to touch the heart of the most indifferent.

Christian visitors are representatives of Christ. They seek to represent Christ to people who know him not. Theirs is a holy mission and requires clean hands, understanding minds, and sympathetic hearts.

(4) *Right methods will get visitation done*

Some suggestions are made as to how a program of continuous visitation may be carried out in any community.

a. Set the example.—No superintendent can lead his workers in a visitation program unless his own heart of compassion is sending him out to visit. He will visit prospective workers and workers who need advice and encouragement. He will go along with other visitors in cases of special need or difficulty. He will visit the lost and the unenlisted.

b. A definite time for visitation is necessary.—The best time possible should be selected and then adhered to. In some communities one afternoon during the week will be best. In many communities Saturday afternoon will be found to be a good time. The majority of people have more leisure time on Saturday afternoon, and this time is near enough Sunday to make the visiting most effective. A good time during Saturday afternoon is usually from four to six or from five to seven o'clock.

The workers may meet at the church building thirty minutes before time to start visiting. The general superintendent should conduct a conference and make sure that everything is ready.

c. Make assignments.—Before starting out from the church building, each worker should know just how many absentees or prospects he is to visit. The absentees in each class should be assigned to the officers and teachers in that class. The general superintendent should have a list of these by classes. It is the well-planned course of action that gets results.

Assignments make the visitation personal. One worker will contact a particular person for a definite purpose. Personal visitation will, as a rule, prove more effective than general visitation. In some homes four to six officers and teachers may visit each week, but that is much better than for only one visitor to go.

Assignments insure a definite purpose for each visit. It may be to secure attendance, to win to Christ, to lead to church membership, to enlist a worker, to make an assignment for some part on a program, to express honest commendation or appreciation, or to visit the sick.

d. Secure reports.—In the weekly officers and teachers' meeting or in the conference just preceding the time for starting on the visitation, reports should be made. It will be helpful for each worker to tell some results of the visits. The report of an absentee brought back, of a prospect won, of someone led to accept Christ, or the report of an unaffiliated Baptist enlisted will bring joy to and intensify the interest of all the workers.

e. Train the workers.—The pastor and general superintendent will have to train the workers to visit. In most churches the habit of visiting has not been formed by the majority of the officers and teachers, and it will require weeks and months of training to get all of them to visit every week. This can be done by the pastor and general superintendent visiting with the workers one at a time, by constant emphasis from the platform, by personal interviews, by example, and by commending those who visit.

It is just as important to train the officers and teachers how to visit as it is to get them to visit. This may be accomplished in the weekly officers and teachers' meeting by reports of successful visits, by demonstrations, and by personal testimonies. A study of the Bible teachings relative to personal work will prove helpful.

Visitation is the method Jesus used. "For the Son of man is come to seek and to save that which was lost." It is the method Jesus has commanded his followers to use. "As my Father hath sent me, even so send I you." It is the method used by the early disciples, "day by day from house to house." It is the method Sunday school workers everywhere must use to build and maintain great Bible schools.

Nearly every Sunday school could add to the average attendance by enlarging the present number of officers and teachers and by carrying on a program of personal, loving visitation. The two people responsible for getting this done are the pastor and the general superintendent. Unless they do it, it will not be done.

The five steps—know the people who ought to be in Sunday school, secure additional workers, provide adequate space, train the workers, and maintain visitation—can be used in any Baptist church.

The difference in Sunday schools is not so much a difference in methods as in the use of these methods. A halfhearted use of the methods brings halfhearted results. Sometimes the methods are blamed for the failure of a Sunday school. However, the failure lies not in the methods, but in the halfhearted use of them. An intelligent, regular, vigorous use of these five steps in building a Sunday school will bring reasonable results in any church.

QUESTIONS FOR REVIEW

1. Give Scripture references showing the teachings of the Bible about numbers.
2. Name the five things a church must do in order to reach people.
3. How may additional officers and teachers be secured?
4. List the methods in getting the Sunday school officers and teachers to visit.

OUTLINE

I. TEACHINGS OF THE BIBLE ABOUT REACHING PEOPLE

    1. God's Desire for Numbers

    2. Jesus' Ministry to Numbers

    3. Churches Commanded to Go after Numbers

II. BIBLE CONCEPTION OF REACHING PEOPLE ESSENTIAL

    1. A Vision of the Unreached Multitudes Needed

    2. A Compassion for the Lost Essential

    3. An Understanding of the Value of a Soul Vital

    4. The Obligation of the Churches Unquestionable

III. A Church Using Its Sunday School to Reach People
    1. Knowing Who Ought to Be in Sunday School
    2. Securing Additional Officers and Teachers
    3. Providing Adequate Space
    4. Training the Workers
    5. Maintaining Regular Visitation

Chapter 3

The Sunday School and Bible Evangelism

I. THE BIBLE THE REVELATION OF GOD TO MAN

The writers of the Scriptures claim the authority of God for their words. Many times in the Old Testament it is said, "The Word of Jehovah came unto me, saying . . ." All through the New Testament one finds an acceptance of the Old Testament as the Word of God—"All scripture is given by inspiration of God" (2 Tim. 3:16). "For the prophecy came not in old time by the will of man: but holy men of God spake as they were moved by the Holy Ghost" (2 Peter 1:21). All the references of Jesus to the Scriptures take their divine origin for granted.

Without the Bible man would not know of the character and personality of God. Something in man tells him there is a God, but without the Bible there he would of necessity stop. The Bible tells man that there is a God and gives his characteristics. It tells man that God created him, that God loves him, that God is able to save him, that God is preparing a home for his eternal happiness. It tells man of the grace of God in complete pardon to every one who will believe. It tells of the grace of God in adopting man into the family of God. It tells man that God has taken him into partnership. It tells man of Jesus, his love, his death, his resurrection, his power. It tells man of the Holy Spirit, his presence in the world, and his purpose in the world. It tells man of himself, his weakness, his sin, his potentialities. The Bible reveals God to man and points man to God.

II. ITS THEME THE PROCLAMATION OF JESUS CHRIST

The promise to fallen man recorded in Genesis refers to Jesus. It is Jesus who gives meaning to the genealogies and chronologies. All the ceremonies of the Old Testament point to Jesus. The prophecies tell of him and his coming. The four Gospels portray his life, work, death, resurrection, and ascension, and prophesy that he is coming again. The Epistles prove the fulfilment of his promises and demonstrate his power. The Revelation pictures his final, complete triumph and tells of his heavenly reign. "Search the scriptures; for in them ye think ye have eternal life: and they are they which testify of me" (John 5:39). "For had ye believed Moses, ye would have believed me: for he wrote of me" (John 5:46). God's answer to the cry of man lost in sin is Jesus. God's only remedy for sin is Jesus. The story of Jesus brings joy unspeakable to groping, bewildered, sinful man.

The Bible is full of Christ from Genesis to Revelation.

III. Its Purpose the Complete Salvation of Man

In John 20:31, the writer tells why the book of John was written:

"But these are written, that ye might believe that Jesus is the Christ, the Son of God; and that believing ye might have life through his name." In 2 Timothy 3:15, Paul gives the result of regular Bible study: "And that from a child thou hast known the holy scriptures, which are able to make thee wise unto salvation through faith which is in Christ Jesus." In 2 Timothy 3:16–17 Paul further says that "All scripture is given by inspiration of God, and is profitable for doctrine, for reproof, for correction, for instruction in righteousness: that the man of God may be perfect, throughly furnished unto all good works."

1. *Man's Sinfulness*

According to the Bible, the heart of man is inherently sinful.

"Behold, I was shapen in iniquity; and in sin did my mother conceive me" (Psalm 51:5). "Among whom also we all had our conversation in times past in the lusts of our flesh, fulfilling the desires of the flesh and of the mind; and were by nature the children of wrath, even as others" (Eph. 2:3).

"For all have sinned, and come short of the glory of God" (Rom. 3:23). "He that is not with me is against me; and he that gathereth not with me scattereth abroad" (Matt. 12:30). "All we like sheep have gone astray; we have turned every one to his own way; and the Lord hath laid on him the iniquity of us all" (Isa. 53:6).

According to the teachings of the Bible, sin is the natural condition of every human heart, and sins are the results. Sin is the root and sins are the fruit. According to the Word of God, sin is on the inside of every heart eating away, and no amount of culture, no perfumed remedies, nor even the highest type of morality will get at the root. Only the power of God can forgive sin, and give power to conquer sins.

2. *Human Efforts Not Enough*

There are those who claim that the individual in the beginning is right with God and all that is necessary is to keep him right. Some say that all that is necessary is to build a moral fence around children and keep sin out. They hold that sin is something caught from the outside, and that if people are kept away from it as fathers and mothers keep their children away from some dread disease, then there is no danger. There are others who claim that culture is the cure for sin. Some say that if the proper education is given the individual, then there is no need for evangelism. Such views are not in harmony with the teachings of the Bible.

According to the Scriptures, no amount of culture, no course of instruction, no system of truths which can be taught, no set of books which can be read can save a soul. "No work of man can change the shade of a sinful soul by so much as a shadow." All these things may be used to bring people under the influence of the gospel and to make Christians more useful, but the Holy Spirit does the work of saving grace. It is obedience, not understanding, that saves. Sin is not a problem to be solved, but an evil to be overcome and only the power of God can overcome sin. No matter how many churches one may join, or how moral one may be, or how many cultural advantages one may have, unless the

Holy Spirit has at some time performed a work of grace, begot a new life, that one is a lost sinner.

When sin becomes so undisturbing and commonplace to Christian workers that it never startles them, then their teaching will become weak and insipid. According to the Scriptures sin is an awful thing. Jesus touched the eyes of the blind and there was physical sight restored. But when he would save a man from the power of sin, he was compelled to go to the cross. When he was dealing with sin, the sun was darkened, the earth was shaken, the veil was rent, and the dead arose. Whoever ignores sin, fails in the most vital place. It takes the wisdom, power, love, mercy, and sacrifice of the Triune God to forgive sin. Christian workers cannot afford to trifle with sin. Just in proportion as they believe that people are lost will they bring them to Christ as the only Saviour. The Pharisees could stand most of the tests ascribed to Christian people today. The Scriptures? They studied them. The creed? They were orthodox to a fault. The church? They were regular attendants upon the synagogue. Prayer? They prayed. Giving? They were even tithers. It was in their attitude toward the lost and needy that they stood exposed. While Jesus was going out after the lost, they pulled their cloaks of self-righteousness about them and critically said, "This man receiveth sinners." Unless Christian workers get God's viewpoint of sin, they can not effectively preach and teach. A proper sense of sin is essential in keeping Christian workers going into the byways and highways. The devil tempted Jesus and tried to turn him away from the cross. The devil is tempting Christian workers today and seeking to turn them away from the cross. Much of the devil's propaganda is so attractive and so reasonable that even the very elect are tempted.

3. *The Only Remedy for Sin*

"And she shall bring forth a son, and thou shalt call his name Jesus: for he shall save his people from their sins" (Matt. 1:21). "Jesus saith unto him, I am the way, the truth, and the life: no man cometh unto the Father, but by me"

(John 14:6). "Neither is there salvation in any other: for there is none other name under heaven given among men, whereby we must be saved" (Acts 4:12).

The Bible reveals God's will and God's love to the lost. Nowhere else except in the Bible is this message of salvation to be found. A study of the flowers, birds, rocks, and trees will not reveal this message. Neither the use of the test tube, the philosophy of men, nor art nor literature will reveal this message. The largest microscope or telescope available will not make known God's plan of salvation or reveal God's love to a lost soul. The gospel of Jesus Christ simply and sublimely stated is the only hope for spiritual triumphs. The early churches were passionately evangelistic churches. They had but one message—Jesus. Their teachings spread like wildfire.

Jesus is still the only way. Nations come and go; things are temporal and soon pass away, but Jesus is the same yesterday, today, and forever. The primary purpose of the Sunday school is to make God's will known to lost and sinning humanity. Sunday school teachers may not know all that they ought to know, but they must know Christ. In learning how to teach, Sunday school teachers must not forget what to teach or why they teach. In all their work, if they are true to the Scriptures, they must put Christ at the center of all they do or teach. The work of the Sunday school is to reach people for Bible study and through Bible study bring them to a saving knowledge of Jesus Christ. The only way to do this is through the use of the Bible.

IV. The Instrument for Evangelism

If the churches are going to have Bible evangelism, they must use the Bible in all evangelistic efforts.

1. *The Holy Spirit Works Through the Word of God*

"But the Comforter, which is the Holy Ghost, whom the Father will send in my name, he shall teach you all things, and bring all things to your remembrance, whatsoever I have said unto you" (John 14:26). "And take the helmet of salvation, and the sword of the Spirit, which is the word of God"

(Eph. 6:17). The Holy Spirit is God present in the world, teaching, seeking, convicting, pleading, saving, guiding, and helping.

2. *Bible Teaching Does Result in Evangelism*

Because of its significance in this connection, 2 Timothy 3:15 is quoted again: "And that from a child thou hast known the holy scriptures, which are able to make thee wise unto salvation through faith which is in Christ Jesus."

In twenty widely scattered churches in several Southern states the records have shown that 93 per cent of the baptisms came from the Sunday school enrolment. If these twenty churches are representative of all the churches, then it is true that the majority of the baptisms come from the Sunday school constituency. This is remarkable in view of the fact that not over 30 per cent of the white population is even enrolled in any Sunday school.

The late Dr. B. V. Ferguson, former pastor, First Baptist Church, Fort Smith, Arkansas, made the following statement: "Probably 90 per cent of the people not in Sunday school are more or less irregular in their church attendance and in all other matters pertaining to the church life. We average two evangelistic services a year here, one led by an outsider and one directed by the pastor. We have observed accurately that 95 per cent of the people reached in all of our revivals are ones who have been first enlisted in the Sunday school. These are not isolated cases. It is an established fact that evangelistic opportunities are found almost exclusively in the Sunday school."

V. THE ONE TEXTBOOK OF THE SUNDAY SCHOOL

Because the purpose of the Bible is the salvation of man, and because the Bible contains the only remedy for sin, then teaching the Bible is of supreme importance.

1. *The Need of All People*

Lost people need the message of the Bible. Creeds will not save. Culture will not save. Tradition will not save. Beautiful surroundings will not save. Ethics will not save. Organization will not save. These things, when rightly used are helpful, but in themselves are powerless to forgive sin or implant eternal life. The hope of people, individually and collectively, is to be found in the Bible.

Saved people need the Bible. Food for the soul is just as essential as is food for the body. The Word of God is the proper food for the soul. The Bible has the living message for every need of the human soul. The safety zone for all people is found in the Bible.

2. *The Obligation of Baptists*

Baptists have said to the world that the Bible and the Bible alone is their sufficient rule of faith and practice. This position obligates Baptists to teach the Bible and to practice its teachings—"to work it all up into Christian experience" and living. Baptists are obligated to teach the Bible to every available individual. To do anything short of this is hypocrisy.

Baptists have set up a high sounding claim and they should substantiate the claim.

In view of the claim of Baptists as to the Bible and the subsequent obligation to teach the Bible, surely they should seek for the best methods and equipment for teaching the Bible. Southern Baptists have developed Sunday school objectives in harmony with the Bible. They have also developed a plan of organization that has demonstrated its value. Their methods of work are resultful wherever they are intelligently used. It behooves the churches to study these methods, install them, and vigorously use them to the end that more and more people may be led to study the Bible and practice its teachings.

3. *The Responsibility of the Churches*

God has trusted the promulgation of his Word to the churches. If the churches are obedient to Christ, they must teach the Word of God. The Sunday school is a church agency for teaching the Word to the masses. The churches must keep the Sunday schools true to the task assigned.

Those who write the Bible lessons for the Sunday school must be true to the Bible. The myriads of Sunday school officers and teachers must be men and women of one Book.

The purpose of the Bible is to magnify Jesus as the Saviour of lost and fallen man. The cross and the empty tomb are central in the Bible and in the work of Jesus. If those who write the Sunday school lessons and if the Sunday school officers and teachers fail God at the vital point of teaching the Bible, they are traitors to the cross of Christ. If they let the devil lead them to substitute something else for the cross, they are traitors to the Lord.

Sunday school workers should bear in mind that if the majority of people are not taught the Bible in the Sunday school, the chances are that they will not be taught the Bible at all. That is true, regardless of age. It is almost absolutely true relative to lost people. The teaching of the Bible has to a large degree been turned over to the Sunday schools. This fact makes it urgent that the churches use the Sunday schools in the largest possible way.

4. *The Foundation of the Sunday School*

Dr. J. M. Frost states in his book, *The School of the Church,* that "the work of the Sunday school is three-fold: First, teach the Scriptures; second, teach the Scriptures; third, teach the Scriptures." The business of a Sunday school is to reach the people and to teach the Bible. Popular topics may be interesting, and many of them may have great ethical values; however, none of them can take the place of the Bible.

The devil is against Bible study. The devil is doing all he can to get the Sunday schools to turn aside from lessons from the Scriptures to lessons on social problems, morals, etc. Sin is the cause. These things are only symptoms and easily discernible. The Bible has the only remedy for sin, and each person needs to know and accept this remedy.

The Sunday school is built upon the Bible. Remove the foundation, and ultimately the Sunday school will fall. Keep the Bible as the foundation, and the Sunday school will continue to grow.

VI. A Sunday School in Action in Bible Evangelism

No apology is necessary for a frequent repetition of reaching, teaching, and winning people. These are the heart and soul of Sunday school work.

1. Reaching the Lost

Wherever the Sunday school has been adequately organized and the organization used, lost people have been reached. There are many lost enrolled in the Junior and Intermediate classes of the Sunday schools. In well-organized and properly functioning Sunday schools, the majority of the Junior and Intermediates have been reached.

Boys and girls are easy to reach for the Sunday school, and churches will be wise to see that the Sunday school is organized and functions to reach all the boys and girls in the community for Bible study. If the Juniors and younger Intermediates are brought into the Sunday school, taught the Bible, and led into the preaching service, a church has an opportunity to win them to Christ.

On the other hand, there are very few lost enrolled in the Young People's and Adult classes. At the first glance this would seem to indicate that the Sunday schools are winning the boys and girls to Christ before they leave the Junior and Intermediate classes. True in part, but in part only. The truth is that Southern Baptist Sunday schools are losing the majority of those enrolled who are not led to Christ before they leave the first two years of the Intermediate age group.

The fact that there are few lost people enrolled in the Young People's and Adult classes is one of the most serious indictments that can be brought against these two groups. The cause for this serious condition is usually a lack of proper administration. Lost Young People and Adults can be reached. Wherever the administrative leaders have organized a sufficient number of classes for Young People and Adults, and then have trained the workers, including the class officers, large numbers of unsaved Young People and Adults have been brought into the Sunday school.

The Sunday school officers and teachers should be led to see that they are responsible for those not enrolled in the Sunday school just as much as for those who are enrolled.

The present churches can reach many lost people through mission Sunday schools. There is a great need for the present churches to foster mission Sunday schools. Baptist churches must accept their responsibility for the people living beyond the church communities. The greatest percentage of lost people are living outside of the areas recognized by churches as their territory. Each church should seek through branch Sunday schools to reach out to a point halfway to the next Baptist church.

2. Teaching the Bible to the Lost

The Bible contains many precious promises for the lost. "Come now, and let us reason together, saith the Lord: though your sins be as scarlet, they shall be as white as snow; though they be red like crimson, they shall be as wool" (Isa. 1:18). "Wherefore he is able also to save them to the uttermost that come unto God by him, seeing he ever liveth to make intercession for them" (Heb. 7:25). "Surely he hath borne our griefs, and carried our sorrows: yet we did esteem him stricken, smitten of God, and afflicted. But he was wounded for our transgressions, he was bruised for our iniquities: the chastisement of our peace was upon him; and with his stripes we are healed. All we like sheep have gone astray; we have turned every one to his own way; and the Lord hath laid on him the iniquity of us all" (Isa. 53:4-6). "For God so loved the world, that he gave his only begotten Son, that whosoever believeth in him should not perish, but have everlasting life" (John 3:16). "That if thou shalt confess with thy mouth the Lord Jesus, and shalt believe in thine heart that God hath raised him from the dead, thou shalt be saved. For with the heart man believeth unto righteousness; and with the mouth confession is made unto salvation. For the scripture saith, Whosoever believeth on him shall not be ashamed" (Rom. 10:9-11). "For whosoever shall call upon the name of the Lord shall be saved"

(Rom. 10:13). These are only a few of the many promises to the lost.

It is the business of the Sunday school to teach the Word of God concerning the lost to those who are not Christians.

The Sunday school workers should study the parable of the sower. The business of the Sunday school worker is to sow the good seed, which is the Word of God. The Holy Spirit is the power, and the Christian worker is the instrument used by the Holy Spirit to plant the Word of God in the mind and heart of the sinner. The farmer prepares the soil and plants the seed, but the power to germinate and cause to grow comes from another source. Just so, the Christian worker cultivates the hearts of people and plants the Word of God, but the Holy Spirit must do the work of regeneration.

The farmer must plant good seed or there will be no harvest. Even so must the Christian worker plant the good seed, which is the Word of God, in order to realize a spiritual harvest.

Sunday school workers should make sure they point sinners to the Lamb of God and not to themselves. A skilful teacher may effectively use the Word of God; but the Word, not the teacher's skill, is the sword of the Spirit. With the Word planted in the heart, the Holy Spirit can break the stony heart. With the Word, the Holy Spirit can open the eyes of the blind and let them see the light of God's saving grace. The gospel is according to the Scriptures, not according to the teacher's wisdom or the teacher's methods.

The fact that the Bible and the Bible alone contains the way of life and the other fact that people who are not in Sunday school do not study the Bible make the work of the Sunday school of the greatest importance. If a church does not use its Sunday school in the largest possible way, the major opportunity for reaching the lost is being neglected.

3. Putting the Lost into the Preaching Service

The Sunday school constituency includes the lost; and large numbers of lost people attend the Sunday schools with some degree of regularity. At the present time there is probably a staggering host of a million or more lost people enrolled in the Sunday schools of the Southern Baptist Convention and hundreds of thousands of unaffiliated Baptists and members of other denominations. How may a church use the Sunday school organization to bring the lost and the "detached" people in the Sunday school into the preaching service?

(1) A right evaluation of the preaching service as a means of winning the lost to Christ is necessary

One of the great needs of Sunday school officers and teachers is to realize the eternal worth of preaching, both for themselves and for their pupils. All of the officers and teachers should have a compassion for the lost and a right evaluation of the preaching service as a place for public confession.

Every individual above Nursery age who attends the Sunday school should hear the Word of God preached. The Beginners and Primaries may sit with their parents for the preaching service. It is of the utmost importance that the Juniors and Intermediates should attend regularly the preaching service. The Young People and the fathers and mothers should have a sense of shame and guilt if they go away just as the preaching service is beginning. When they do go away, by their example they are saying to the lost people and to the boys and girls that they do not feel a need for the preaching service or that they count it of little value.

The pastor will be conscious of the evangelistic opportunity as he prepares his message for the preaching hour. There will be many Junior boys and girls in the preaching service as well as others who need a Saviour.

(2) The pastor's attitude determinative

The pastor's attitude should be one of love, interest, and co-operation toward the Sunday school. It seldom does any good for a pastor to criticize the Sunday school officers and teachers who do not attend the preaching service. Not many of them will respond to criticism. They will get enough of that elsewhere. Sunday school officers and teachers will respond to love, sympathy, guidance, and instruction. Sunday school officers and teachers are human beings with human frailties. However, the majority of these workers will follow the pastor's leadership if he will love them, instruct them, and lead them.

Personal conferences with teachers relative to the salvation of the lost in their classes will help to build the preaching attendance.

(3) Build the Sunday school in rural churches

In most rural churches, all those who come to the Sunday school usually remain for the preaching service. Many no doubt have not thought of the necessity of the Sunday school in rural churches as a means of building the preaching attendance. However, the preaching attendance in rural churches will increase in proportion to the increase in the Sunday school attendance. Therefore, the pastors in the rural churches will find the opportunities to reach the lost with the gospel increasing as they lead in building the Sunday school.

4. Officers and Teachers Winning the Lost

The Sunday school officers and teachers constitute a company of personal soul-winners. They have a continuous, intimate, and vital opportunity to win the lost. An opportunity is afforded through constant association through a period of months and sometimes years. There is the opportunity of personal contact which is effective and essential in winning the lost. The opportunities to do personal work are many. There are the opportunities during the week in the regular visitation, in the class meetings, in the socials, and in definitely planned-for contacts. There are the opportunities on Sunday before Sunday school opens, during the Sunday school hour, and in the worship service. Perhaps the most effective means of getting lost people to attend the preaching service is personal work on the part of the officers and teachers. The intimate relationship of pupil and teacher makes possible personal contact with the parents in the interest of boys and girls who are not Christians.

QUESTIONS FOR REVIEW

1. Give the purpose of the Bible.
2. Give the main thought in what Dr. B. V. Ferguson said about the Sunday school as an evangelistic agency.
3. Why are Baptists obligated to teach the Bible?
4. Discuss the Sunday school in action in Bible evangelism.

OUTLINE

I. THE BIBLE THE REVELATION OF GOD TO MAN

II. ITS THEME THE PROCLAMATION OF JESUS CHRIST

III. ITS PURPOSE THE COMPLETE SALVATION OF MAN
   1. Man's Sinfulness
   2. Human Efforts Not Enough
   3. The Only Remedy for Sin

IV. THE INSTRUMENT FOR EVANGELISM

V. THE ONE TEXTBOOK OF THE SUNDAY SCHOOL
   1. The Need of All People
   2. The Obligation of Baptists
   3. The Responsibility of the Churches
   4. The Foundation of the Sunday School

VI. A SUNDAY SCHOOL IN ACTION IN BIBLE EVANGELISM
   1. Reaching the Lost
   2. Teaching the Bible to the Lost
   3. Putting the Lost into the Preaching Service
   4. Officers and Teachers Winning the Lost

Chapter 4

The Sunday School and Enlistment

I. THE NEW TESTAMENT TEACHING OF ENLISTMENT

What is the New Testament meaning of enlistment? In all Christian work the individual is central. Jesus places great value upon the individual. Jesus was supremely interested in the inner growth of the individual. The leaders of his day were satisfied with outward conformity. He asked for inner righteousness as well.

There are four distinct phases of Christian enlistment taught in the New Testament—the idea of growth, the doctrine of stewardship, the principle of service, and the practice of giving. A brief study is given to the four phases, taking them in their order.

1. Includes the Idea of Growth

Enlistment as taught in the New Testament means first of all the growth of the individual Christian. Christian growth means growing in Christlikeness.

The Scripture teaching of Christian growth is definite and clear. "For the kingdom of heaven is as a man travelling into a far country, who called his own servants, and delivered unto them his goods. And unto one he gave five talents, to another two, and to another one; to every man according to his several ability; and straightway took his journey. Then he that had received the five talents went and traded with the same, and made them other five talents. And likewise he that had received two, he also gained other two. But he that had received one went and digged in the earth, and hid his lord's money. After a long time the lord of those servants cometh, and reckoneth with them. And so he that had received five talents came and brought other five talents, saying, Lord, thou deliveredst unto me five talents: behold, I have gained beside them five talents more. His lord said unto him, Well done, thou good and faithful servant: thou hast been faithful over a few things, I will make thee ruler over many things: enter thou into the joy of thy lord. He also that had received two talents came and said, Lord, thou deliveredst unto me two talents: behold, I have gained two other talents beside them. His lord said unto him, Well done, good and faithful servant; thou hast been faithful over a few things, I will make thee ruler over many things: enter thou into the joy of thy lord. Then he which had received the one talent came and said, Lord, I knew thee that thou art an hard man, reaping where thou hast not sown, and gathering where thou hast not strawed: and I was afraid, and went and hid thy talent in the earth: lo, there thou hast that is thine. His lord answered and said unto him, Thou wicked and slothful servant, thou knewest that I reap where I sowed not, and gather where I have not strawed: thou oughtest therefore to have put my money to the exchangers, and then at my coming I should have received mine own with usury. Take therefore the talent from him, and give it unto him which hath ten talents. For unto every one that hath shall be given, and he shall have abundance: but from him that hath not shall be taken away even that which he hath" (Matt. 25:14-29).

"That we henceforth be no more children, tossed to and fro, and carried about with every wind of doctrine, by the sleight of men, and cunning craftiness, whereby they lie in wait to deceive; but speaking the truth in love, may grow up into him in all things, which is the head, even Christ" (Eph. 4:14-15).

"That I may know him, and the power of his resurrection, and the fellowship of his sufferings, being made conformable unto his death; if by any means I might attain unto the resurrection of the dead. Not as though I had already attained, either were already perfect: but I follow after, if that I may apprehend that for which also I am apprehended of Christ Jesus. Brethren, I count not myself to have apprehended: but this one thing I do, forgetting those things which are behind, and reaching forth unto those things which are before,

I press toward the mark for the prize of the high calling of God in Christ Jesus" (Phil. 3:10–14).

It is a serious blunder for a church to consider the newborn Christian as being full grown. It is also a tragedy for the individual Christian to get such a conception. After regeneration, the work of developing spiritual babes into full-grown spiritual men and women by the use of the Word of God is the most important work of a church.

There are many examples in the New Testament illustrating Christian growth. The growth of the apostles in the Christian graces is an example of the possibilities of the Christian life. The man with five talents gained five more. The man with two talents gained two more. It is clear that the man with one talent could have gained one more if he had applied himself as the man with the five talents and the man with the two talents did.

No doubt, there are many illustrations in the reader's own church and among his acquaintances showing marvelous Christian growth and development. But there are multitudes of lives being wasted through misuse and neglect.

Many times there comes the cry, How much does the denomination lose? But the individual is forgotten. The cry, How much does the individual lose? is equally important. A New Testament church is made up of individuals with individual responsibilities. The task of a church is to help each individual to develop a symmetrical Christian life. A deep yearning for service is latent in the soul of every child of God. "No man hath hired me," sets forth the condition of a multitude of Christians.

It seems reasonable that if churches would give personal attention to the enlistment of every member in Bible study and Christian service, there would be less trouble in securing workers and money for the work at home and abroad and fewer cases of arrested spiritual development.

2. Teaches the Doctrine of Stewardship

New Testament stewardship teaches that God is the owner and that man is the steward.

(1) *God is the owner*

"What? know ye not that your body is the temple of the Holy Ghost which is in you, which ye have of God, and ye are not your own? For ye are bought with a price: therefore glorify God in your body, and in your spirit, which are God's" (1 Cor. 6:19–20).

"Every good gift and every perfect gift is from above, and cometh down from the Father of lights, with whom is no variableness, neither shadow of turning" (James 1:17).

New Testament stewardship includes the conception of God as the Creator and Owner of all things. It also includes faith in God as the all-wise, all-powerful, all-merciful, all-loving God.

(2) *Man is the steward*

"As every man hath received the gift, even so minister the same one to another, as good stewards of the manifold grace of God" (1 Peter 4:10). "He said therefore, A certain nobleman went into a far country to receive for himself a kingdom, and to return. And he called his ten servants, and delivered them ten pounds, and said unto them, Occupy till I come."

New Testament stewardship takes in all of life—time, talents, influence, possibilities, possessions, personality—all one is or can be. No doubt many church members think of stewardship as a burdensome sacrifice, giving away something or parting forever with what belongs to one. New Testament stewardship is just the opposite. New Testament stewardship means that God gives to each individual capital—life, abilities, opportunities, personality—and power to use the capital. The New Testament teaches that God blesses the efforts of the steward and gives the increase; and then God permits the steward to use whatever increase results (Matt. 25:14–30).

New Testament stewardship provides an opportunity for a Christian to make a safe and profitable investment of life, all of life. A right conception and practice of New Testament stewardship safeguards a Christian against the waste of time, talents, possessions, opportunities, and possibilities.

There is no loss of real values in a proper practice of New Testament stewardship. The Christian has everything to gain and nothing of value to lose in being a good steward of God. Happiness, growth of soul, contentment, wider opportunities, and love of God (God loves a cheerful giver), and an eternal reward are some of the values of good stewardship.

A right practice of stewardship brings the joy and thrill Paul had when he said, "I have fought a good fight, I have finished my course, I have kept the faith: Henceforth there is laid up for me a crown of righteousness, which the Lord, the righteous judge, shall give me at that day: and not to me only, but unto all them also that love his appearing" (2 Tim. 4:7–8).

The underlying principle of stewardship is "Give, and it shall be given unto you; good measure, pressed down, and shaken together, and running over, shall men give into your bosom. For with the same measure that ye mete withal it shall be measured to you again" (Luke 6:38).

It is quite evident that Christians generally have not yet learned the beauty, glory, and value of New Testament stewardship. Giving is not all of New Testament stewardship. Intelligent giving is a result of stewardship. New Testament stewardship is beautiful and glorious in its fellowship and partnership. It is also invaluable in that it presents opportunity for a profitable and safe investment of life.

3. *Embraces the Principle of Service*

"Go ye therefore, and teach all nations, baptizing them in the name of the Father, and of the Son, and of the Holy Ghost: teaching them to observe all things whatsoever I have commanded you: and, lo, I am with you alway, even unto the end of the world. Amen" (Matt. 28:19–20).

"I beseech you therefore, brethren, by the mercies of God, that ye present your bodies a living sacrifice, holy, acceptable unto God, which is your reasonable service" (Rom. 12:1).

"For whosoever will save his life shall lose it: but whosoever will lose his life for my sake, the same shall save it" (Luke 9:24).

"But it shall not be so among you: but whosoever will be great among you, let him be your minister; and whosoever will be chief among you, let him be your servant: even as the Son of man came not to be ministered unto, but to minister, and to give his life a ransom for many" (Matt. 20:26–28).

The blessed privilege of Christian service is one of the plainest doctrines of the New Testament. It is found on almost every page of the New Testament.

The heart of Christianity is service. "For even the Son of man came not to be ministered unto, but to minister, and to give his life a ransom for many" (Mark 10:45).

Every Christian is divinely obligated to give of his time in service. The giving of sums of money at stated intervals does not take the place of the personal service of a life. A man who ought to be teaching a class of boys in the Sunday school or leading a Training Union cannot fulfil the personal obligation by giving a few extra dollars from his income. Christian service is a personal matter, just as salvation is a personal matter.

In all Christian service there is the reflex blessing—give and ye will receive; lose and you will save; plant and you will reap; cast your bread upon the waters and it will return. These are blessed promises contained in the Word of God.

New Testament stewardship includes giving the devotion of the heart and the service of the life. When this is done, one comes to find sweet fellowship and deep satisfaction in giving and serving.

Christian people can give of their time in personal efforts. There are many attractive avenues open for men and women to give of their time, such as teaching a Sunday school class, working in a Training Union, putting forth personal efforts to win the lost, and many others. Christ in the heart of an individual puts the "must" of John 9:4 into a life: "I must work the works of him that sent me, while it is day: the night cometh, when no man can work."

4. *Commands the Practice of Giving*

"I have shewed you all things, how that so labouring ye ought to support the weak, and to remember the words of the

Lord Jesus, how he said, It is more blessed to give than to receive" (Acts 20:35).

"But this I say, He which soweth sparingly shall reap also sparingly; and he which soweth bountifully shall reap also bountifully. Every man according as he purposeth in his heart, so let him give: not grudgingly, or of necessity: for God loveth a cheerful giver" (2 Cor. 9:6–7).

"Now concerning the collection for the saints, as I have given order to the churches of Galatia, even so do ye. Upon the first day of the week let every one of you lay by him in store, as God hath prospered him, that there be no gatherings when I come" (1 Cor. 16:1–2).

Stewardship finds its practical expression in serving and in giving. If a Christian is right on the New Testament conception of giving, he is usually right in most spiritual responsibilities.

Christians need to give, not alone to meet the many needs, but for the spiritual development of their own lives. They need to give to keep from becoming selfish and covetous. The interest, love, and devotion of men and women, boys and girls is of great importance. God wants men more than money. The story of the rich young ruler is an example of this. Jesus' desire was not for his money. Jesus wanted to deliver this fine young man from the clutches of his wealth and set him free for larger and finer things. A man is not compelled to give in order to become and remain a member of a church. He must give to keep his soul from becoming selfish and covetous. "It is more blessed to give than to receive."

There is no ultimate happiness in getting and holding. Christians find growth of soul, peace of mind, and happiness of heart in yielding all to God, in regular study of the Bible, and in unselfish, generous giving of self and means.

II. SOUTHERN BAPTISTS AND NEW TESTAMENT ENLISTMENT

What does the word "enlistment" mean as used by Southern Baptists? Enlistment as used by Southern Baptists has to do with attitudes toward and participation in all the work of the kingdom of God by individual Christians and churches.

The Bible and the Bible only is the standard for Baptist churches. Jesus and Jesus only is the Lord of his people. However, it is vain for Baptists to make the claim that the Bible is their sole authority and that Jesus is the Lord and Master of every Christian life and of every Baptist church unless they strive earnestly to practice the whole teachings of the New Testament and unless they obey Jesus and try to "do all the things which he has commanded."

No doubt, the demands have influenced churches and agencies to take short cuts in an effort to secure money without first making adequate efforts to prepare the minds and hearts of those giving the money. It may be that churches and agencies in many instances have "picked" all they could get, and have in a large measure failed to fertilize, water, and cultivate. Such an attitude places the major emphasis of enlistment upon getting money. Is it not a fact that if the proper fertilizing and cultivating are done, fruit will be a natural result? Much is written and said about enlistment being the greatest weakness of Southern Baptists. This weakness, no doubt, goes back to the failure to train and develop the individual.

When Southern Baptists measure their enlistment efforts and achievements by the New Testament teachings, they find a woeful neglect.

1. A Woeful Neglect

In view of the fact that, within the bounds of the Southern Baptist Convention territory, there were in a certain year some thirty-five million white people not in any church, almost forty-five million not enrolled in any Sunday school, several hundred Baptist churches which did not contribute to missions, and other thousands which went for a whole year without reporting a single baptism, it would seem that some of the churches are not practicing fully the teachings of the New Testament.

(1) Consider the conditions of the churches

During any given year there will be several thousand of the churches which report no baptisms.

Several hundred other churches report only one baptism each.

Thousands of churches give nothing to missions and benevolences.

Other thousands of churches give only to the orphans' homes.

The local expenses of many of the churches claim the large share of every dollar contributed.

There is only one baptism to every twenty members of the average church.

(2) *Consider the individuals in Southern Baptist churches*

About 40 per cent of the church members are regular church attendants.

Less than one half give anything for the local expenses of the churches.

An even smaller number give to any missionary, educational, or benevolent cause.

Only one of five has any definite work in the churches.

The per capita gifts of all Southern Baptists for all purposes are only about $24.00 a year.

The per capita gifts for all missions, education, and benevolences are less than $5.00 a year.

Almost 40 per cent of the members in the best churches, taken as a group, are not even enrolled in the Sunday school, to say nothing of attending it.

2. *A Serious Condition*

It is a serious condition for several thousand churches to go for twelve months without winning even one person to Christ! The churches with the least organization show the least spiritual power. The churches which do not report a single baptism and the churches which have no sort of organization, not even a Sunday school, are spiritually dead or dormant churches.

Again, it is a serious condition for several thousand churches to go for a whole year without contributing one penny to outside causes. And in practically all of these very little was given even to local expenses. Where were the pastors, deacons, Sunday school superintendents, teachers, clerks, treasurers?

Why is it that several thousand Baptist churches did not report even one penny to missions for a whole year? The most of them had pastors. No doubt they all had deacons. The most of them had Sunday school superintendents and Sunday school officers and teachers. The reason any church goes a year or a month or a week without giving to missions is first of all because the leaders—pastors, deacons, and Sunday school officers and teachers—do not give to missions. Many of the church members will respond if the leaders will set the example and provide an opportunity for the members to give. The leaders hold the purse strings. They may not hold all of them, but they do hold their own, and they do keep many of the church members from giving to missions by their failure to provide opportunities for such giving. They also have much to do with where the money goes that is given.

Think of a pastor's going for a year and not giving anything to missions or leading a church to give one penny to missions! Think of the deacons in a church going for a whole year and not giving to missions or leading the church to give to missions! What are they doing? Think of the Sunday school officers and teachers going for a year and not giving anything to missions! How can they teach the Bible and not practice its plain teaching?

Again, think of three or four million Southern Baptist church members going for a whole year and not giving one penny to missions—and the majority of them not giving much, if anything, to local church expenses.

Are these leaders—pastors, deacons, Sunday school workers, other church officers, and members—able to give? In a certain year Southern Baptists averaged $7.50 per capita to missions. In the same year the per capita spending for tobacco was more than $32.00. If you are one of the few who do not use tobacco, note that the per capita outlay for pleasure riding is enormous. If you do not spend for the items named, perhaps you are a participant in one of the following luxuries:

chewing gum, cold drinks, picture shows, baseball, and beauty parlors. Do the things Christians spend their money for indicate what they love? If so, please notice that Southern Baptists spend over four times as much for tobacco as for missions. In a certain year, a merchant in a big rural community reported that the Baptist church members in that community spent over $2,000 annually for tobacco. The amount reported for missions by the Baptist church in that community was not 15 per cent of $2,000.

If Southern Baptist pastors, Sunday school officers and teachers, and Training Union leaders would work as faithfully, intelligently, and attractively to get the nearly seven million Baptist church members to understand and practice New Testament stewardship as the tobacco companies do to get these same church members to use tobacco, what do you suppose would happen? This discussion does not deal with the ethical side of the tobacco question. The question is raised, however, as to the right of Southern Baptists to spend six times as much for tobacco as they do for missions.

3. *A Great Opportunity*

However, there are many encouraging features relative to Southern Baptists and enlistment. Southern Baptists are potentially immensely rich. They are rich in the number of churches. Southern Baptists have 30,000 churches, and they are reasonably well distributed. If the present Baptist churches and especially the larger ones could be led to see the need and to accept the task, they could through the organization of mission points establish a Baptist work in every needy community.

They are rich in the number of church members. Southern Baptists have over eight million church members. Nearly three fourths of these are not really enlisted in service or giving. Thousands of these church members are idle because no man hath hired them.

Southern Baptists are rich in enlargement opportunities. There are ever-increasing millions of people in their territory who are not now in any Sunday school of any denomination. Since Southern Baptists have approximately one fourth of the white Sunday school enrolment, it is reasonable to assume that one fourth or more of the unreached people are Baptist responsibilities.

Southern Baptists are rich in evangelistic needs. The fact that there are thousands of lost people enrolled in Southern Baptist Sunday schools is proof that the lost people can be reached. The South, Southwest, and West are among the richest, ripest, and most promising mission fields in the whole world so far as Baptists are concerned. These fields must be worked and made to produce the means for extending the gospel to the uttermost parts of the earth.

III. THE SUNDAY SCHOOL AN EFFECTIVE MEANS OF ENLISTMENT

The Sunday school is ideally suited for enlistment.

1. *The Sunday School a Church Agency*

The officers and teachers are elected by the church. The work of a Sunday school is assigned by the church. The Sunday school is a church organized for reaching people, teaching the Bible, winning the lost, and developing and enlisting the church members. The extent and work of a Sunday school as a church enlistment agency is limited only by the use made of it by the church of which it is a part.

2. *Provides a Place of Service for Large Numbers of People*

It is possible to provide in a Sunday school a place of attractive, worth-while service for the majority of the church members. In a Sunday school is an ideal place for the individual Christian to work. Here the individual may find an opportunity for fellowship, study, Christian growth, and Christian service. Here the individual can multiply his efforts through co-operation with his fellow laborers.

A church can provide in its Sunday school a place for each individual to study the Bible. A church can also provide in its Sunday school a place for each individual Christian to develop his talents.

If pastors and Sunday school superintendents will begin organizing the Sunday school to meet the distinct needs of individuals, no doubt large classes will be divided into smaller groups so as to make possible individual attention; additional classes will be started to provide places for men and women to develop their God-given talents, some as teachers, some as administrative officers, some as personal workers.

The basic principle in organizing a Sunday school should be to meet the spiritual needs of individuals, such as conversion, growth in spiritual life, and enlistment in service. Mr. Arthur Flake, in speaking of the Sunday school status, says this: "In this organization every member of the church may find a suitable place of service. Here may be found the pastor's most fruitful field for utilizing the entire membership in helpful, attractive service for Christ." Considering teachers, general officers, department officers, and class officers, the opportunities for using individuals are limited only by the vision, ability, and spirit of the pastor and general superintendent.

Many capable Christian workers testify that they did their first Christian work in a Sunday school. Many pastors had their first experience as Christian workers as Sunday school teachers or as Sunday school superintendents. Teaching a Sunday school class or acting as a Sunday school officer has been a spiritual blessing to many Christian men and women.

3. Ministers to the Individual

The Sunday school is conducted for the good of the individual. The need of the pupil determines the type of organization. The lessons are planned for the individual. The building is erected for the individual. There are several contributing factors which magnify the individual.

(1) The Sunday school is closely graded

The Sunday school is graded on the age basis. In even the small school there will no more than four years in any one class up through the Intermediate group, if the school is graded. In many Sunday schools there is a class for each sex and each age in the Junior and Intermediate groups. Churches are coming to establish more classes for Young People and for Adults. Because of the close age grouping it is possible to prepare graded material and adapted lessons. The regular Sunday school lessons are filled with Bible teachings concerning enlistment. These can be used to help each class member find an avenue of service suited to his ability.

(2) *Close grading and small classes magnify the individual*

One of the major reasons for small classes is to make possible individual attention with each pupil. Organizations are not for the sake of organizations, but for the purpose of providing a place to win, use, and develop individuals. Some men decry organization. Some pastors and superintendents are burdened with maintaining organizations. Have they seen only a machine and worried themselves sick looking for individuals to complete an organization? If they will begin studying the organization for a place to develop and use individuals, no doubt joy will take the place of worry, privilege will be substituted for drudgery, Christian character will become the end, and organization the means to that end.

A church is not really adequately organized until a place has been provided for each individual to study the Word of God, and to develop the talents which God has given him.

In many churches there are not one-half enough classes of Young People and Adults to minister to the church members in these two groups, not to mention the lost people and the unaffiliated Baptists.

(3) *The Sunday school has the individual from birth through adulthood*

Through the Sunday school officers and teachers a church can begin with the children in the impressionable years and help to make the trends of life lean toward New Testament stewardship. The Sunday school has the pupil at each stage of development. As the pupil advances in age he is promoted from one class to another. The Sunday school has a place for the individual throughout the whole of this life. Enlistment includes the idea of growth, and growth requires time. Christian stewardship, Christian service, and generous and wise giving must be made a real part of a life. To do this requires time. The opportunity for individual enlistment through the Sunday school is tremendous because of its lifelong contacts with each person.

Because the Sunday school is a church agency, because so many of the church members can be used in the Sunday school, and because through close grading and small classes the Sunday school ministers to the individual for the entire span of life, a church will find in its Sunday school an effective enlistment opportunity.

IV. USING THE SUNDAY SCHOOL IN ENLISTMENT

Four practical ways are suggested whereby a church may use its Sunday school in New Testament enlistment:

1. In Developing the Individual

Thirteen things are mentioned that a Sunday school can do for each individual. The officers and teachers in the various classes should be led to understand that the Sunday school exists for the individual. They should also understand that the Sunday school is seeking to minister to the individual at each stage of his development. No one class may be able to do all of the thirteen things suggested, but all the classes working together can do all of them for each individual.

> Reach the individual.
> Hold the individual.
> Teach the Bible to the individual.
> Lead him to attend the preaching service.
> Win him to Christ.
> Lead him to join the church.
> Enlist him in the Training Union.
> Teach him to pray without ceasing.
> Guide him in his reading.

Help him in the selection of a school.

Encourage him to be a personal soul-winner.

Enlist him in some definite Christian work in the church.

Enlist him in scriptural giving.

2. *In Teaching Stewardship*

A Sunday school superintendent should study and practice New Testament stewardship, instruct his officers and teachers, and lead them to practice the New Testament teachings. Through the teachers, through the class officers, and through the worship programs a church can inform all of its members and provide frequent opportunities for them to give. The books on stewardship and missions in the training courses for Sunday school workers and Baptist Training Union workers can and should be used by pastors and superintendents.

3. *In Enlisting in Missions*

How can a church use its Sunday school in missionary enlistment? The means and opportunities are unlimited. The methods are many and in reach of every church. Some practical means are suggested whereby any church may use its Sunday school in enlisting in missions.

(1) *By praying for missionaries and mission causes*

Every one of the over eight million church members can have a part in the spread of the gospel to the uttermost parts of the world through united earnest prayer. It may be that much of the praying in public is general. Should it not be definite? The pastor, Sunday school superintendent, and teachers should bring before the people definite objects of prayer.

(2) *By teaching mission study classes*

Surely, every church should have at least one mission study week each year. The Sunday school officers and teachers should be enlisted in all such schools. In small churches the pastor could bring together all the officers and teachers from every department of the church and teach a book on missions.

Where necessary, several classes may be provided. Are many of the church members doing as well as they know? An intelligent study of conditions will show the Sunday school officers and teachers the needs, warm their hearts, and bring the smoldering fire of love and devotion to a leaping flame. Missionary information will beget missionary interest.

(3) *By reading missionary books and periodicals*

It is possible to have a library in every Baptist church in the Southern Baptist Convention. Not only is it possible, but positively necessary if the needs of the people are to be met. A church library should contain a good selection of missionary books. The pastor and superintendent can use the Sunday school organization to get the books read by as many people as possible. The church librarian has a great opportunity to permeate the whole church life with the spirit of missions.

Many worth-while periodicals, denominational papers, missionary tracts, and much free literature are available. Missionary literature can be had from any of the general or state boards of the denomination. The pastor and superintendent should urge the Sunday school officers and teachers to subscribe for the denominational paper and should see that missionary tracts are available and widely used.

(4) *By observing special days*

At least four mission causes should be presented by the Sunday school each year. Home and foreign missions in March, state missions in October, the ministry of the Children's Homes in November, hospitals in May, and many other special emphases may be used to give up-to-date missionary information and inspiration. The Committee on Denominational Calendar each year prepares a calendar showing the special missionary emphases to be promoted by the denomination. *The Sunday School Builder* carries programs for Home and Foreign Missions Day and State Missions Day. From time to time it also features other causes in assembly programs in the various department sections.

(5) *Through the regular Sunday school lessons*

The missionary emphasis can be found in practically every lesson. The pastor and general superintendent should take advantage of the weekly officers and teachers' meeting to call attention to the missionary truths in the lesson and to urge that they be stressed. The teacher has an opportunity to keep the missionary appeal constantly before the class.

Good Bible teaching is a source of missionary inspiration. The untaught Christian is rarely a missionary Christian. Surely, a church can do nothing which will mean more in missionary emphasis and in missionary practice than teaching the Word of God to all the people.

(6) *By making the Sunday school programs missionary*

Assembly periods—general or department—and, in many rural churches, the time after the lesson period offer the leaders frequent opportunities for presenting missionary information. Carefully prepared programs on missionary subjects should be presented frequently.

(7) *Through co-operation with other church organizations*

The Baptist Training Union presents a great opportunity to instruct and enlist the church members in missionary activities. Through the Woman's Missionary Union organizations an opportunity is presented to inform and enlist the women of the church. The Baptist Brotherhood has as its aim to enlist all the men in the whole denominational program.

Much good can be done with the Sunday school, Baptist Training Union, Baptist Brotherhood, and Woman's Missionary Union organizations all co-operating in the plan of a Unified Budget, and teaching and training all the members of the church and congregation to give to the whole church and denominational program.

4. *Through a Plan of Weekly Giving*

Any full-time, half-time, or fourth-time church can use the Sunday school organization in an effort to enlist each member of the congregation to make a weekly pledge, and then can use this Sunday school organization to make it possible for these pledges to be paid each Sunday.

This plan does not and should not take the matter away from the church. The church, through the pastor and regular officers, should nominate a budget committee, preferably made up of three regular church officers. The church, through the budget committee, should have the direction and supervision of the work.

It seems that church utilization of the Sunday school organization is one open, practical, and sure way of developing the small as well as the large churches in a financial program. The churches meet every Sunday in the capacity of a teaching service. Many of them meet once a month for a preaching service. The church can function every Sunday through the Sunday school organization in Bible study, in worship, in missionary emphasis, and in scriptural giving. The pastor with fourth-time preaching is necessarily absent from the field most of the time, and he must find a way to develop his churches. The Sunday school offers this opportunity.

A plan of weekly giving, if rightly used, will help multitudes of Christian men and women to grow in the Christian graces. Is it true that a preacher is sinning against his people if he fails to advocate strongly, intelligently, and patiently scriptural giving? Is it also true that he is sinning against the great multitude of lost people who are waiting for someone to bring the gospel to them? Furthermore, is it true that the deacons are failing to do their duty when they fail to provide practical, definite plans whereby all the people may have an opportunity to give?

QUESTIONS FOR REVIEW

1. What are the four phases of enlistment taught in the New Testament?
2. Discuss Southern Baptists and New Testament enlistment.
3. Why is the Sunday school an effective enlistment agency?
4. How can the Sunday school be used in enlistment?

OUTLINE

I. THE NEW TESTAMENT TEACHING OF ENLISTMENT
1. Includes the Idea of Growth
2. Teaches the Doctrine of Stewardship
3. Embraces the Principle of Service
4. Commands the Practice of Giving

II. SOUTHERN BAPTISTS AND NEW TESTAMENT ENLISTMENT
1. A Woeful Neglect
2. A Serious Condition
3. A Great Opportunity

III. THE SUNDAY SCHOOL AN EFFECTIVE MEANS OF ENLISTMENT
1. The Sunday School a Church Agency
2. Provides Places of Service for Large Numbers of People
3. Ministers to the Individual

IV. USING THE SUNDAY SCHOOL IN ENLISTMENT
1. In Developing the Individual
2. In Teaching Stewardship
3. In Enlisting in Missions
4. Through a Plan of Weekly Giving

Chapter 5

The Pastor Leading the Sunday School

I. THE PASTOR'S OPPORTUNITY IN THE SUNDAY SCHOOL

The opportunity offered in the Sunday school for promoting the work of a church, when understood, will bring to the heart and mind of a pastor a sense of confidence, comfort, certainty, and courage. This is particularly true in churches with part-time preaching. A Sunday school offers an effective way of promoting much of the work of a church. The Sunday school organization can be expanded to any size the church will make it, thus providing a large number of regular, interested workers. As a church agency, the Sunday school organization can be used in any task a church has to do. The Sunday school, if wisely and energetically used, pays a pastor great dividends on the investment made.

1. *Proper Evaluation of the Sunday School*

There are three prevailing attitudes toward the Sunday school on the part of the pastors. First, there are the pastors who ignore or simply tolerate the Sunday school. The Sunday school is usually a disappointment when such is the case. Although in no way to blame, yet the Sunday school is often criticized for the failure to accomplish the things it is supposed to do. Second, there are the pastors who place the major emphasis upon the social implications of the gospel, and still others whose major appeal is to the esthetic and cultural side of life. A Sunday school finds a minor place in such churches because the first aim of a Sunday school should be Bible evangelism. Third, there are the pastors who recognize in the Sunday school their most resultful means of reaching the lost for Bible study and for the preaching service. Wherever this attitude prevails, the possibilities for using the Sunday school in winning the lost are tremendous.

2. Using the Sunday School to Know the Constituency of the Church

The Sunday school offers the pastor a means of knowing the constituency of a church. He may not be able to keep in touch with each individual church member or with each individual enrolled in the Sunday school, but he can keep in touch with the officers and teachers and through them keep in constant touch with each person enrolled. The pastor can use the Sunday school organization to locate and to keep in constant touch with all those who are not members of the church or Sunday school. Through a constant use of the Six Point Record System, the weekly officers and teachers' meeting, regular visitation, and a regular census, a pastor can have reliable, useful, workable information about every individual in a church community. In securing information about the constituency for a church, the pastor will find a properly functioning Sunday school his most effective and resultful agency.

3. Using the Church Members in the Sunday School

A properly functioning Sunday school is a church agency that a pastor can use effectively to find a place of service for the church members. In the Sunday school the pastor can use almost any number of capable men and women. Many of the church members can be used as officers, teachers, personal workers, musicians, and in special tasks. In many churches, numbers of the members can be used in mission Sunday schools. Some churches conduct as many as six, and some even more, separate mission Sunday schools. The Sunday school serves a twofold purpose in that it provides places of service for many church members and at the same time provides an army of workers.

4. Putting the Sunday School to Work at the Task of the Church

The Sunday school is regularly engaged in the missionary work of a church—enlargement, Bible teaching, evangelism, and enlistment. A pastor who yearns to reach more people for Christ should consider the Sunday school as a resultful means. A pastor who is seeking places of service for church members should study and build his Sunday school. A pastor who is eager to keep the work of the church centered upon Bible study, evangelism, and enlistment should make the greatest possible use of the Sunday school. The Sunday school offers a pastor one of the surest and safest ways of promoting the work of a church.

Of course, a pastor can watch the Sunday school organization from afar and commend the work of the officers and teachers when he visits the classes. However, there is a great difference in saying a few complimentary words from the platform and in actually assuming the responsibility of leadership imposed when called by the church to be pastor.

Sometimes the statement is made that a pastor does not have time to lead the Sunday school officers and teachers. It is not a question of time, but of the wisest and most profitable use of time. In this instance the question is, Will a pastor lead a church to accomplish more of the work it is responsible for doing by making a major use of the Sunday school? The experience of many pastors proves that he will.

If the Sunday school has seemingly failed as a church agency, the fault is not with the Sunday school but with the use of it. If a pastor assumes his rightful place of leadership, masters Sunday school objectives and methods, and puts the officers and teachers to work at any task the church ought to do, he will be agreeably surprised at both the response and the results. Such leadership requires preparation, time, and effort. A pastor need not expect the officers and teachers to take the work of a church seriously and positively unless he himself accepts the Sunday school as a church agency, assumes the place of leadership which is rightfully his, and actually leads in doing the task assigned.

II. The Pastor's Responsibility for the Sunday School

1. Some Wrong Conceptions

(1) The pastor has not become adept at Sunday school work

The statement is sometimes made by pastors that they are not adept at Sunday school work. Personalities and aptitudes differ with men. Also, some men have more physical endurance than others. However, a pastor should feel himself at ease in any department or class in the Sunday school, and will if he masters the purpose and the possibilities of the Sunday school. There are many pastors who are excellent workers in many ways, but seem to be ill at ease in the Sunday school. A lack of preparation and experience may be the cause for this attitude.

(2) The work of a Sunday school is not deemed worth the pastor's consideration

There are others who claim that the work in the Sunday school is not worth the consideration of a pastor. Such a conception of the teaching of the Bible is most unfortunate and, of course, detrimental to the whole church program. Teaching is a vital part of the Great Commission. Paul called himself a teacher, and made use of teaching as a major method of doing the Lord's work.

(3) The physical demands are considered too great

Again, some pastors do not take part in the Sunday school, saying that it makes too great a physical demand upon their strength. No doubt a preacher should be at his best for the preaching hour. It is not necessary for the pastor to teach a class on Sunday morning. He may, if he desires and if it seems wise. It is usually better for the pastor to give his attention, interest, and sympathy to all of the Sunday school on Sunday morning. There are many things a pastor can do during the Sunday school session that will better prepare him for the preaching hour. A wise pastor will find where he is most needed and will do all he can to direct and encourage the Sunday school. Much of a pastor's work with the Sunday school will be done during the week in the weekly officers and teachers' meeting, in the training schools, through personal conferences, through a study and use of the Sunday school records, and in other ways.

2. *The Pastor the Chief Leader of the Sunday School*

Dr. William E. Hatcher, great denominational leader of the past generation, in his book *The Pastor and the Sunday School,* said: "A minister who cannot thoroughly identify himself with his Sunday school ought not to be a pastor. Unfitness for service in this cardinal branch of Christian activity amounts to a disability. To be useless in that department of church work which has to do with the study of the Scriptures and with the salvation of the young is to offer an overwhelming argument against one's worthiness of a pastoral charge."

If a church ought to teach the Bible to the masses and if the Sunday school is an effective agency for reaching people for Bible study, then the pastor's obligation to the Sunday school is very definite. A pastor who does not direct the Sunday school is usually headed for trouble.

3. *The Pastor Obligated to Know Sunday School Work*

If a pastor is going to direct a Sunday school, he should know Sunday school work. A doctor has as much right to perform delicate operations without knowing the human body as a pastor has to direct a Sunday school without knowing Sunday school work. In fact, there is no reason why a pastor should not know Sunday school work. The experience of other pastors has been recorded in books and literature, and this information is available at small cost for any one who will secure and study it. A pastor can have no optional attitude toward the Sunday school. The Sunday school is a church agency, and the pastor is the chief leader; and therefore, he does bear the chief responsibility for the Sunday school.

III. The Pastor's Work in Leading the Sunday School

We come now to study the delightful work of a pastor leading his Sunday school forces.

1. *In All Its Work*

If the Sunday school officers and teachers are constant in their efforts to reach more people, the pastor will have to see that the Sunday school organization is adequate and that regular visitation is carried on. If a Sunday school takes seriously its work of teaching the Bible, the pastor will have to see that the officers and teachers understand that the Bible is the one textbook of the Sunday school and see that they are trained for their task. If the Sunday school is positively and primarily evangelistic, the pastor will have to see that the officers and teachers have a passion for the lost and that practical plans are adopted and carried out. Whether the Sunday school is aggressively missionary or not will be determined by what the pastor does in his relationship to the Sunday school. Whether or not there is a spirit of loyalty to the church will be determined by the leadership of the pastor. If the Sunday school officers, teachers, and pupils attend the preaching services in large numbers, the pastor will have to win their respect, love, and co-operation.

Too long have Sunday school classes been left to define their own activities without consideration of the spiritual needs of the individuals enrolled or the work and program of the church. All too often the classes were not at fault. No direction had been given by the church. Their work had not been outlined and carefully defined. Quite often classes have kept all the offering received each Sunday morning, giving perhaps a small portion to the church. Where this is being done, the Sunday school is not recognized as a church agency, and as a rule does not measure up to its highest possible efficiency.

Increasing emphasis on department oversight of classes is improving this situation, but nothing can eliminate the need for a pastor's active leadership.

The pastor who has no time to give to the Sunday school officers and teachers should not be surprised when some of the classes and departments fall short in their conception of the purpose of the Sunday school and also in their attitude and co-operation with the work of the church.

2. *In Creating and Maintaining the Right Spirit*

Nehemiah 4 : 6 reads: "So built we the wall; and all the wall was joined together unto the half thereof: for the people had a mind to work." Why did the people have a mind to work? Because Nehemiah the leader had the spirit to work. Nehemiah's statements to the people were words of encouragement, "Come let us build up the walls of Jerusalem that we be no more a reproach." Again we hear him encourage the people with these words, "The God of heaven, he will prosper us." Fortunate is the pastor who can keep the Sunday school officers and teachers happy, eager, and determined in their work.

Elisha asked Elijah for a double portion of his spirit. Christian workers everywhere need to have a double portion of the spirit of enthusiasm, faithfulness, work, patience, courage, and many other Christian virtues. A right spirit is a great possession. A Christian who has lost his spiritual fervor is like salt that has lost its savor. One peril of a Christian is that he may lose his spirit. When a Christian loses his spiritual glow, he has lost his power, his driving force. One's words will be colored by the state of his mind. One's acts will largely be controlled by the inner attitude. A pastor should watch his own spirit, and then watch the spirit of the Sunday school officers and teachers.

Pastors and superintendents are engaged in a work that when properly presented will challenge the best in real men and real women.

A man speaking to a group of men, reaching his climax, shouted: "You can lead a horse to water, but you can't make him drink," as he waved his hand in a gesture of finality!

"Salt him," drawled a man in the rear of the building who knew horses.

Just so, many times it has been said that you can organize a class, but you cannot get the teacher and class officers to work. If the leaders will provide a little encouragement, set a worthy example, speak some words of honest commendation, hold some personal conferences, establish some worthy objectives, conduct some training schools, carry on a weekly officers and teachers' meeting—some of these efforts will be the means of kindling the spark of interest in the hearts of the officers and teachers and also of prospective officers and teachers.

3. *Through the Superintendent*

As far as possible the pastor should see that the best available person is elected as superintendent. The pastor is fortunate indeed to have a good man as superintendent. It will be a good investment to cultivate him and guide him. If a pastor accomplishes very much, he will have to work through others. He will not be concerned about who gets the credit, but rather about the development of his people and the accomplishment of the work assigned to the church. The pastor should magnify the work of the superintendent and the superintendent should magnify the work of the pastor. The pastor should have frequent conferences with the superintendent. The plans of the Sunday school should be discussed and the pastor and superintendent should be in hearty accord before any suggestion is made to the officers and teachers. The pastor should support the superintendent in his efforts to get the work of the Sunday school done. The pastor and superintendent should be "buddies" and co-laborers. Quite often pastors are heard to use the expressions "my church," "my superintendent." Sunday school superintendents resent this attitude on the part of the pastor. The pastor should feel toward and speak of the superintendent as a co-laborer. If he does, the superintendent will appreciate it, feel keenly his responsibility, and work hard to justify the pastor's confidence in him.

4. *In the Selection of the Officers and Teachers*

Because of the work of the Sunday school; because of the importance of Bible teaching; because of the possibilities of the Sunday school as an evangelistic agency; because of the importance of the right kind of officers and teachers; because of the position of the pastor, he should lead in the selection of the officers and teachers.

(1) *This requires constant effort*

It requires continuous effort on the part of pastor and superintendent for a church to have uniformly good Sunday school officers and teachers.

A valuable executive in an important business concern died. In twenty-four hours an equally capable man was on the job made vacant by the death. And thus might vacancies be filled in most Sunday schools if Sunday school leaders put forth continuous efforts to select, enlist, and train present and prospective workers.

The cry, We can't get capable Sunday school officers and teachers, might possibly be changed to, We haven't made the work of selecting, enlisting, and training the Sunday school officers and teachers a major interest.

(2) *Enlist the youth*

It is well to take account of the youth in the selection of workers. If the task of enlisting and training Sunday school officers and teachers is postponed until after marriage and active business, the work of enlistment will be more difficult.

Right-minded young people want to serve. The interest and zeal of youth is cause for rejoicing. If the desire to serve is stifled in youth, it will be difficult to stir it up in adulthood. One peril of waiting until people are mature to enlist them in Christian service is loss of zeal and enthusiasm. Unless people learn to work for the Lord while they are young and the heart is eager and open, it is doubtful if many of them will learn after maturity. Then there are the perils of the cares of the world and the responsibilities of family and business.

Perhaps if a pastor will lead a church to use the youth when they desire to serve, the adulthood will respond when there is work to do. It is dangerous to discourage youth when the desire to serve is manifested, and it is surely disastrous to doubt their capacity or ability to serve. Young people are open-minded and are willing and eager to learn. They do not come to the task with preconceived ideas. With reasonable efforts young people can be taught the possibilities of Sunday school work and the best methods of doing it.

Young people make excellent Sunday school workers, just as they make good workers everywhere. They need not do all of the work in a Sunday school, but it will be well to keep placing them in the organization for their own good and for the future success of the Sunday school.

And as for Bible study and Christian growth, young people will do more Bible study and develop faster as teachers than they will as pupils.

(3) Begin with people as they are

Jesus took Peter, James, John, Andrew, and the others just as they were. He knew what he wanted them to be. He poured his divine life into them. He patiently changed their conceptions. He lovingly informed and guided them until they finally came to see the spiritual significance of the kingdom of God. Pastors and superintendents need not expect perfection of the Sunday school officers and teachers to begin with. Leaders who are capable of recognizing their own weaknesses and limitations will be sympathetic with their co-workers. It is not necessary to condone low standards of conduct or work on the part of Sunday school officers and teachers. The methods of helping them should be to love, guide, inspirit, and commend.

If a pastor will be the friend and co-laborer of the officers and teachers, they will be his friends and co-laborers. Good Sunday school officers and teachers are not born but made—made out of the men and women in the churches.

Many pastors and superintendents know that it is difficult to find capable, loyal Sunday school officers and teachers. It is indeed difficult, but it is profitable and it is glorious. It has been difficult to find and train capable workers ever since Jesus selected the twelve and for three years taught them, but it is necessary and it is profitable.

It is perhaps no more difficult for pastors and superintendents to get teachers than it is for teachers to get pupils. The teachers are "fishers of men," and the pastor and superintendent are "fishing for fishers." The methods of securing officers and teachers are discussed in chapter 2.

5. *In the Training of the Officers and Teachers*

(1) *Jesus set the example*

Jesus gave the major portion of the three years of his public ministry on earth to the training of his disciples. Now and again he withdrew from the throngs to be with his disciples. He wanted his work to go on after he left. He not only gave the major portion of his time to the training of the twelve, but commanded them to pray for other workers. In his commission, one of the things he commanded was to teach them to observe all things whatsoever he had told them. Paul expressed the idea when he said "The things that thou hast heard of me . . . the same commit thou to faithful men, who shall be able to teach others also" (2 Tim. 2:2).

(2) *Workers need training*

Many faithful, willing Sunday school officers and teachers have not had the advantages of college or seminary training; neither do they have the time for exhaustive Bible study that the pastors have. All workers need the stimulation and growth which regular training provides. By teaching books in the training course for Sunday school workers, the pastor can instruct, strengthen, and encourage the teachers in their work of teaching the Bible. He can develop prospective workers.

The Sunday school gives the pastor an opportunity to teach the Bible regularly to the largest possible group of people. Much of the teaching will have to be done through the officers and teachers, but in this way, the lessons and teaching can be adapted to the needs and capacities of the individual.

(3) *The pastor is responsible*

The pastor will have to accept the responsibility of training the teachers in what to teach and how to teach if a church is to have uniformly good Bible teaching. A pastor with two or more churches may not be able to conduct all of the training classes a church should have, but he will be able to plan for them and see that they are held. A pastor will desire to teach directly as far as he is able, but he can accomplish much more through the Sunday school officers and teachers. Dr. J. M. Frost in his book, *The School of the Church,** has a chapter on "The Pastor and His College of Teachers." It is a picture of the church school with the pastor as the teacher of the officers and teachers. There are a number of books in the Sunday School Training Course offering the best that is known about every phase of Sunday school work. A church should have four or more training schools each year.

Perhaps the most effective way for a pastor to make permanent progress is to teach and train the workers in the churches. It may seem to be a slow way, but it is nevertheless a sure and resultful way.

6. *In the Use of Right Methods*

Through the years Southern Baptists have developed some practical and resultful Sunday school methods. These methods have been tried and proved in a large number of churches. They are the best known methods for Southern Baptist Sunday schools. The methods are adaptable in all situations. They are just as practical and resultful in the small Sunday schools as in large.

The pastor will find it profitable to lead, perhaps through the superintendent, in the organization of new classes. He will want to see that the Sunday school is graded. He will desire to lead in planning for and promoting regular visita-

* Out of print.

tion. He should see that a good weekly officers and teachers' meeting is conducted; that a good system of records is installed and used; that the Standard of Excellence is adopted by the church and used as a program of work for the Sunday school; and that a sound financial system is used.

The adoption and active, vigorous use of right methods of Sunday school work will keep a Sunday school growing and improving the quality of work being done.

Reference is made to the books, *Building a Standard Sunday School, Sunday School Officers and Their Work, The True Functions of the Sunday School, The Six Point Record System and Its Use* and *One to Eight* for a fuller study of the right methods of Sunday school work.

QUESTIONS FOR REVIEW

1. Discuss the pastor's opportunity in the Sunday school.
2. Why is the pastor responsible for the work of the Sunday school?
3. In what ways may the pastor lead the Sunday school?
4. Where can the pastor secure additional officers and teachers?

OUTLINE

I. THE PASTOR'S OPPORTUNITY IN THE SUNDAY SCHOOL

    1. Proper Evaluation of the Sunday School

    2. Using the Sunday School to Know the Constituency of the Church

    3. Using the Church Members in the Sunday School

    4. Putting the Sunday School to Work at the Task of the Church

II. THE PASTOR'S RESPONSIBILITY FOR THE SUNDAY SCHOOL

    1. Some Wrong Conceptions

    2. The Pastor the Chief Leader of the Sunday School

    3. The Pastor Obligated to Know Sunday School Work

III. THE PASTOR'S WORK IN LEADING THE SUNDAY SCHOOL
1. In All Its Work
2. In Creating and Maintaining the Right Spirit
3. Through the Superintendent
4. In the Selection of the Officers and Teachers
5. In the Training of the Officers and Teachers
6. In the Use of Right Methods

Chapter 6

The Position and Work of the Superintendent

IF A SUPERINTENDENT makes a success in leading in the accomplishment of the work of a Sunday school, he must have the right attitude toward his position, accept the responsibility for leading the Sunday school, understand what a Sunday school should be and do, and then know how to get the work done in the most effective way.

I. AN OPPORTUNITY FOR THE INVESTMENT OF A LIFE

What shall I do with my life? is a question most men ask at some time. Better perhaps it is for a Christian man to change the question to: Lord, what will thou have me to do? When Paul asked that question, the will of God was revealed to him step by step.

God has given one or more talents to each person. God expects each person to use the talents. Every worthy person desires to use his life in the most profitable way. Every Christian desires that the will of God shall be done in his life.

There are many avenues of service open to Christian men and women today whereby they may minister to mankind. Is the Sunday school a good investment? Is it a good investment of time? Will it pay? These and similar questions must be answered by thoughtful Christians who are asked to assume the responsibility of leading a Sunday school. The Sunday school offers the superintendent a great opportunity for making a safe and profitable investment of his own life. The Sunday school superintendent who thinks of his work merely as a contribution to others has only a partial conception of his position. His position offers him not only an opportunity for helping others, but for making a wise investment of his own life and for laying up an eternal reward.

Week by week as busy men and women do the work of Sunday school officers and teachers, they can make a safe and profitable investment of time, thought, energy, love, example —yea, and many other lasting values.

The opportunities in Sunday school work for the investment of a life are limitless. The individual worker will determine the extent of the investment and something of the quality of the investment from the standpoint of the worker. The silent investment of influence, the invaluable investment of well-chosen words, and other unseen, but nevertheless real, values are open to a Sunday school superintendent.

In addition to the silent unseen values, there are many practical ways whereby a superintendent may make profitable and lasting investments.

1. *Enlisting a New Teacher*

Enlisting a new teacher is a profitable way for a superintendent to make an investment. When the Sunday school superintendent of Walnut Street Baptist Church, Louisville, Kentucky, enlisted a teen-age girl as a teacher, little did he dream that a few years later that person would be with one of the larger denominations in the South as editor of the Uniform Lesson quarterlies for the Beginner, Primary, and Junior groups, numbering 80,000 officers and teachers, and 800,000 boys and girls.

In a church in Arkansas a superintendent enlisted a new teacher. In eighteen months the teacher enlisted sixty-three pupils. In a church in Oklahoma a superintendent enlisted a young woman as teacher, and in one year's time the teacher enlisted more than thirty pupils.

If a Sunday school superintendent is looking for an opportunity to make a profitable investment, let him enlist a Sunday school teacher, give the teacher a list of prospects and a place to meet, and help the teacher succeed. He who enlists a new pupil may save a soul from death and a life from waste; but he who enlists a good teacher may save a score of souls from death and win a number of lives for Christian service.

2. *Organizing a New Class*

The organization of a new class may prove to be a most profitable investment. In a church in Tennessee a Sunday school superintendent had a conference with a young businessman who was a member of the church but who had no definite responsibility. The superintendent asked the young businessman to accept the task of building a class for a group of young men who were not in Sunday school. The task was accepted and after months of hard work on the part of the teacher and superintendent the class that had started with only potentialities came to be a glorious reality. This class has functioned for years. Scores of young men have been enrolled in this class during its history. If it continues to function, scores of others will come under this spiritual influence. If it takes six months or even a year to build a new class, it is worth all the effort.

3. *Reaching a New Pupil*

The enlistment of a new pupil frequently proves to be a most profitable investment. Dr. Roland Q. Leavell, in his book *Winning Others to Christ* tells the following story:

"Years ago a lady found a German boy by the name of Myers on the streets of Louisville, Kentucky. She asked him, 'Would you not like to attend Sunday school tomorrow?' He said that he would. Later she asked, 'Would you not like to become a Christian?' He said that he would. Again she asked, 'Would you not like to live in my house and go to school?' He said that he would. Years later she asked, 'Would you not like to be a preacher and go to the seminary?' He said that he would. At last, she asked, 'Would you not like to go to Japan as a missionary?' He said that he would, and he did. This same missionary, Dr. W. H. Myers, led Toyohiko Kagawa to Christ. Little did the good woman in Louisville know she was starting a stream of spiritual blessing which would exalt Christ in Japan and throughout the world. When she invited that boy to Sunday school, she did her greatest deed in life. The soul-minded missionary multiplied his life by thousands.

Win a boy to Christ and it may mean winning a continent. It is life's highest privilege and opportunity."

4. *Organizing a New Sunday School*

The organization of a new Sunday school is yet another way for a Sunday school superintendent or any Sunday school officer or teacher to make a profitable investment.

In 1924 Rev. J. H. Reynolds organized a mission Sunday school in the west part of Little Rock, Arkansas. Yes, there success seemed remote. In 1936 Tabernacle Baptist Church had special services to dedicate a Sunday school annex. The church at that time had 1,000 members, 900 enrolled in Sunday school, and during 1936 baptized 122 people. Brother Reynolds stated that he considered the organization of the mission Sunday school out of which grew Tabernacle Church one of the major investments of his life. No doubt, this church will go on ministering to the spiritual needs of people in increasing numbers. Where could a Christian find an opportunity for a more profitable investment?

5. *Providing a Vacation Bible School*

The Vacation Bible school offers an opportunity for every Sunday school superintendent to make a profitable investment, with a minimum of time and expense.

The Round Island Church in the Limestone Association, Alabama, held a Vacation Bible school with eighty enrolled. There were thirteen conversions during the school, though it lasted only ten days.

In one church in the Mount Zion Association in North Carolina there were 146 enrolled in the Vacation Bible school and 19 conversions. In a larger church in Oklahoma there were 920 enrolled and 145 conversions.

In a "mushroom" community of Baltimore, Maryland, where there was no Baptist church, a Vacation Bible school was held in 1943. From this beginning sprang Middle River Baptist Church, one of the most active in the city.

II. AN OPPORTUNITY FOR CHRISTIAN SERVICE

The opportunity of a Sunday school superintendent for service is wide, even to the limits of the community and beyond. He has the opportunity of working with the pastor in building a strong Bible-teaching, soul-winning, giving church. His opportunity is limited only by his ability, spirit, and willingness to study and work.

There are many privileges in life which men seek and to which they give their best.

A doctor has a wonderful privilege in being able to cool fevered brows, stop intense pain, bind up ghastly wounds, and straighten crooked limbs. The Sunday school superintendent has the privilege of introducing sin-sick, sin-crippled, and sin-doomed men and women, boys and girls to the Great Physician who has the power to give eternal life. The teacher has the marvelous privilege of instructing boys and girls, of developing their minds, of teaching them how to study, of acquainting them with the best literature and the greatest minds of all ages, and of preparing them for citizenship in this world. The Sunday school superintendent has the exalted privilege not only of helping men and women to prepare themselves for citizenship here but for eternity. The merchant has the privilege of providing people with food to sustain life here. But the food which he provides will last for only a few hours. The Sunday school superintendent has the privilege of offering people the Bread of life. The architect has the privilege of erecting beautiful buildings, but they soon decay and are no more. The Sunday school superintendent has the privilege of building Christian character which endures throughout eternity.

The work of the Sunday school superintendent deals with eternal verities.

A Sunday school superintendent has the privilege of seeing that the Bible, the Book of books, the Word of God, the message of salvation, is taught to every available individual. He has the privilege of seeing the vast majority of all the lost people who are held in the Sunday school for any reasonable length of time accept Christ as their Saviour. He has the privilege of helping people grow in the Christian graces and of enlisting them in Christian service. He has the privilege of changing the conceptions of people from self to others, from mammon to God, from sin to salvation, from doing little things to undertaking great things. Surely, such a task should challenge men to rigid faithfulness, intelligent preparation, godly living, sacrificial giving, and hard work. An opportunity bestowed upon real men always produces a spirit of genuine humility, deep gratitude, and a determination to give one's best.

There is nothing under heaven greater than winning people to Christ, and that is what a Sunday school superintendent is leading a church to do.

III. THE SUPERINTENDENT'S PLACE OF LEADERSHIP

The Sunday school superintendent may well ask himself these questions: Am I a leader? What are the evidences of my leadership? Is the Sunday school any larger than when I was elected? Do I know where I am going? If so, do I know how to get there? Do I know how many are enrolled in the Sunday school? Do I know WHO is enrolled in the Sunday school? Do I know how many people should be in this Sunday school? Do I know how many new people joined the Sunday school during the past year? Do I know how many of them are now enrolled? Do I know how many of the church members are enrolled in the Sunday school? Do I know how many lost people are enrolled in the Sunday school? How many people have accepted Christ and joined the church from the Sunday school during the past year? Do I know what the teachers are teaching? What have I done during the past year in an effort to improve the Bible teaching and Bible study in the Sunday school?

The superintendent of a Sunday school is elected by the church. The church elected him to find out the best methods of getting the largest possible number of people to study the

Bible regularly. The church expects him to lead in the work of the Sunday school. The election of a Sunday school superintendent carries with it the responsibility to lead.

The superintendent should know what is to be done, and then stand for it, advocate it, and make plans for bringing it to pass. A good superintendent will keep abreast of the best in Southern Baptist Sunday school methods and plans, and will be ever alert and active in giving the people in his church the best. It is his task to find out what is best; bring it to his people; show them the advantage of what he knows is right; and then lead them to appropriate it to themselves and use it for the good of the work.

The Sunday school superintendent should be a man of action. He must make the attack. If there be indifference, a good superintendent will overcome it by his interest. If there be ineffective methods in use, he will tactfully show a better way. If there be a lack of spiritual fervor, he will set the example by his dedication of life and talents. Whatever needs to be done, let the superintendent take the lead, mark out the way, and plead for and bring about the co-operation of all the officers and teachers. If he will find the right way, and then faithfully stand for it, the people will sooner or later understand and follow.

IV. THE WORK OF THE SUPERINTENDENT

Along with the joys and privileges of being a Sunday school superintendent there will be burdens to bear and hard work to do. Surely the superintendent will accept the obligations imposed. There is the task of using the Sunday school to build the church of which it is a part. It is his duty to keep the Sunday school growing. There is the obligation of Bible teaching. There is the task of creating and maintaining a soul-winning atmosphere. There is the work of enlisting in regular giving all those who attend the Sunday school. His responsibility is to make the Sunday school doctrinally sound, positively evangelistic, and aggressively missionary, both at home and unto the uttermost parts of the earth. Let's study in order the work of a Sunday school superintendent.

1. *To Make the Sunday School Build the Church*

The purpose of the Sunday school is to build the church of which it is a part.

(1) *The superintendent should see that the Sunday school is properly related to the church*

The superintendent should see that all of the Sunday school is properly related to the church and its work. He should be a loyal and active member of the church. He is a church officer, elected by the church, and responsible to the church. The Sunday school is a church agency. The work of the Sunday school is defined and assigned by the church, and the superintendent is responsible for seeing that the Sunday school, all of the Sunday school, does the work assigned by the church and only the work assigned by the church.

The superintendent should lead the officers and teachers to understand that they, too, are officers of the church, elected by the church, assigned to some definite task by the church, and that they are responsible to the church.

He should also lead the church to see the possibilities of the Sunday school as a church agency. He should lead the church to support the Sunday school with material equipment and supplies and also with the attendance of the church members.

Sometimes the accusation is made that the Sunday school organization does not co-operate with the church. The church should assume the responsibility for the direction and use of the Sunday school. The Sunday school is a powerful and effective church agency, and the superintendent should see that the Sunday school, all of the Sunday school, is put back of the work of the church and that the Sunday school does the work assigned to it by the church.

(2) *He should put the Sunday school into the preaching service*

In practically all rural Sunday schools the problem is not one of putting the Sunday school attendance into the preaching service, but of building the Sunday school attendance. However, every Sunday school superintendent should make preaching attendance of those who are in the Sunday school one of his major emphases. The following means will aid in building the preaching attendance:

The Unified Service
The Six Point Record System
The weekly officers and teachers' meeting
Personal conferences with officers and teachers
Personal work by the officers and teachers
Example of each officer and teacher

2. *To Keep the Sunday School Growing*

Every Sunday school should grow. It is the task of the Sunday school superintendent to see that the Sunday school does grow. It is a serious matter for a Sunday school to go for a year and fail to grow. A Sunday school should grow because there are so many people not in Sunday school. It should grow because people ought to study the Bible. It should grow because it cannot fulfil its ministry unless it reaches the people who ought to be in Sunday school. It should grow because the population is increasing rapidly. Every Sunday school should grow.

Growth does not come as a result of standing still, by leaving things just as they have always been. Growth comes by division. Consider the bees. A farmer starts with one stand of bees and in a few years has twelve stands. They all came from one stand. Consider the flowers. A woman starts with one plant and in a few years has many plants in her own yard and has supplied her neighbors with cuttings. They all came from the same plant. Consider a city. It starts from two or three houses. A new street is opened, a subdivision is started, a new store is organized, and thus the city grows.

Consider the Baptist churches. A revival meeting is held in a schoolhouse, and a church is organized; or a mission Sunday school is started and later a church is organized. Consider a Sunday school. It is organized with three classes and an attendance of thirty. Later there are forty workers with an attendance of 250. Growth in a Sunday school as in all of life comes by division. It is the business of the superintendent to keep the Sunday school growing. He can do this by organizing additional classes and departments and by promoting regular visitation, and by wise administration.

3. *To See That the Bible Is Taught*

The textbook of the Sunday school is the Bible. The purpose of the Sunday school is to teach the Bible. The business of the Sunday school superintendent is to see that the Bible is used by every officer, teacher, and pupil in the Sunday school. The church elected the superintendent for the purpose of getting the Bible studied by every available individual. The task of the superintendent is to get all of the people to study the Bible all of the time.

Many superintendents claim that it is hard to get the teachers to use the Bible. Of course if the teachers do not use it, the pupils will not. The devil knows that if lost people really study the Bible it will "make them wise unto salvation through faith which is in Jesus Christ." Also he knows that if saved people study the Word, it will "keep them from sin" and be a "light unto their path and a lamp to their feet." If the devil can keep Sunday school superintendents from being positive about the regular use of the Bible, he is going to do it. Sunday school leaders should not let the devil use them to keep a Sunday school from really using the Bible. Here as in everything worth while it is simply a matter for honest and continuous efforts.

(1) *The Sunday school makes possible regular Bible study*

The plan of the Sunday school makes regular Bible teaching possible. The Sunday school meets every Sunday, year after year. The Bible lessons are adapted to the different age groups. If a Sunday school functions properly in its organization, in its visitation, and in its administration, each individual who is enrolled will have an opportunity to study the Bible regularly for all of his life on this earth. Beginning with the Cradle Roll work and continuing through the Extension work, a place is provided in a Sunday school for each individual year by year.

The suggested daily Bible readings provide the general superintendent with an attractive plan for promoting regular, related, adapted daily Bible reading. Whether the Uniform or Graded Lessons are used, the superintendent could lead the entire school to use the daily Bible readings as given with each lesson. If necessary, the references could be printed on cards and paid for by the church. He may also provide honor roll charts on which the names of all those reading these parallel passages could be placed.

(2) *Southern Baptist Sunday school methods promote the use of the Bible by officers, teachers, and pupils*

a. The Six Point Record System suggests Bible in hand.— The Six Point Record System suggests that every officer, teacher, and pupil should have a Bible in hand every Sunday. Every Sunday school pupil should have a Bible of his own. By an intelligent, vigorous use of the Six Point Record System the superintendent can within a short time lead all the pupils to secure Bibles. Nearly always the parents will provide Bibles for themselves and their children if they have the necessary encouragement. Where they cannot afford it, the superintendent should see that the church gives them Bibles. In some schools the church presents a good Bible to each pupil entering the Junior classes either as a new pupil or on Promotion Day. The Six Point Record System encourages the bringing of Bibles to Sunday school by each officer, teacher, and pupil.

b. The Standard of Excellence requires the use of the Bible.—The Standard of Excellence requires the use of the Bible in the Sunday school. When the Standard of Excellence is adopted and the school is regularly checked by it, it is revealed to what extent the Bible is being used.

c. The weekly officers and teachers' meeting promotes Bible study.—The weekly officers and teachers' meeting is the place where the superintendent can see that the officers and teachers use the record system and thus encourage each pupil to bring the Bible. In this meeting he can show them how the Bible can and should be used in the Sunday school and also lead them to use it. In a modern Sunday school, where else is the superintendent going to know what is being done? How is he going to know what is being taught unless he has his teachers in a weekly officers and teachers' meeting and hears them teach and instructs and trains them in the Bible teachings.

d. The Sunday School Training Course emphasizes the Bible.—The purpose of the Sunday School Training Course is to encourage the Sunday school to reach more people for Bible study and to help the officers and teachers do the most effective teaching. All of the books on Sunday school administration magnify the Bible as the textbook of the Sunday school. There are a number of books on the Bible in the training course. A constant and intelligent study of these books will tend to keep Sunday school officers and teachers using the Bible.

(3) *The annual Vacation Bible school provides extra Bible study*

A Vacation Bible school is one of the important phases of Sunday school work in that it makes available two full weeks of extra Bible study in a church. The plan is to conduct a Bible school for at least ten days for three hours each day, five days a week, during the period when the public schools are closed. As far as possible, the officers and teachers for the Vacation Bible school should be the regular Sunday school officers and teachers. However, if for any reason they cannot serve, then others will have to be enlisted. The young people home from college for the summer, public school teachers, and other capable young people can do this work in an excellent manner.

The Vacation Bible school presents a major opportunity for some much-needed extra Bible study. The pastor and superintendent should ask the church to vote to make the Vacation Bible school a part of the Sunday school. The superintendent should accept the responsibility for this work and see that the church has an annual Vacation Bible school.

Free literature and all needed supplies can be had by writing to the state Sunday school secretary or to the Sunday School Department of the Baptist Sunday School Board, Nashville, Tennessee.

4. To Make the Sunday School Positively Evangelistic

The primary purpose of the Bible study in the Sunday school is evangelism. The Sunday school can be used to reach the lost, teach the Bible, and put the lost into the preaching service. If these three practical things are done by the Sunday school officers and teachers, the pastor will have a perennial opportunity to preach to the lost. The superintendent can through regular visitation, an annual census, and the organization of new classes, reach the lost. Through the use of the Standard of Excellence, the Six Point Record System, the weekly officers and teachers' meeting, frequent training schools, and the assembly program periods, he can secure the use of the Bible and build the preaching attendance. The superintendent should seek in every possible way to create a soul-winning atmosphere.

The superintendent's attitude, spirit, and example toward the lost will have much to do with the evangelistic atmosphere and attitude throughout the Sunday school organization. A Sunday school worker without compassion for the lost is like a watch without a spring.

5. To Make the Sunday School Doctrinally Sound

The superintendent should see that every teacher and officer believes the Bible and practices its teachings. Certainly every man has a right to his doctrine. No one questions that right. Baptists have always stood for individual rights. However, this individual privilege does not include the right to teach in a Baptist church. The business of the Sunday school superintendent is to protect the people as well as to provide for them. He should protect classes from individuals with unscriptural ideas and pet hobbies. He is obligated as a

church officer to see that all the officers and teachers are positively, aggressively, doctrinally sound. He can do this through
a careful selection of the officers and teachers. He can see that
the doctrinal books in the training course for Sunday school
workers are taught at regular intervals. He can use the weekly
officers and teachers' meeting to insure scriptural teaching.

6. *To Make the Sunday School Aggressively Missionary*

The superintendent should be aggressively missionary. If
the superintendent is missionary in word and in deed, his
spirit and his example will permeate and guide the officers
and teachers and through them the Sunday school pupils.

The superintendent should work constantly to make the
Sunday school aggressively missionary in its teaching. He
should also lead the Sunday school to be aggressively missionary in supporting missions in the local community, in the
state, and throughout the world. The Cooperative Program
makes this possible.

He should see that the officers and teachers are missionary
minded. The superintendent should co-operate with the Baptist Training Union in his church. He should also co-operate
with any and all mission study classes, leading the officers and
teachers to attend.

He should pray, and lead the officers and teachers to pray,
for the missionaries and their work. This can be done in the
weekly officers and teachers' meeting, in the assembly programs, and in the departments and classes.

The superintendent can see that the Sunday school is missionary in its teaching by teaching missions through the regular lessons, by presenting the mission causes through the
worship programs, by an intelligent use of the Calendar of
Denominational Activities, by giving strong emphasis to the
special missionary days, through a wide and intelligent use
of missionary literature, by a wise use of the Standard of
Excellence, through the weekly officers and teachers' meeting, and in many other practical ways.

He should encourage the church to start mission Sunday
schools wherever they are needed. Such missions may be in

outlying sections or for the Negroes or any foreign group that may be living in or near the community. Southern Baptist churches have a wonderful opportunity and a heavy obligation with the Negroes and foreigners in their midst. Through mission Sunday schools is perhaps the most effective way to begin a spiritual ministry with these groups.

QUESTIONS FOR REVIEW

1. Discuss the Sunday school as an opportunity for the investment of a life.
2. Why is the superintendent's place one of leadership?
3. Outline the work of the superintendent.
4. What are some results which may come from a Vacation Bible school?

OUTLINE

I. AN OPPORTUNITY FOR THE INVESTMENT OF A LIFE
1. Enlisting a New Teacher
2. Organizing a New Class
3. Reaching a New Pupil
4. Organizing a New Sunday School
5. Providing a Vacation Bible School

II. AN OPPORTUNITY FOR CHRISTIAN SERVICE

III. THE SUPERINTENDENT'S PLACE OF LEADERSHIP

IV. THE WORK OF THE SUPERINTENDENT
1. To Make the Sunday School Build the Church
2. To Keep the Sunday School Growing
3. To See That the Bible Is Taught
4. To Make the Sunday School Positively Evangelistic
5. To Make the Sunday School Doctrinally Sound
6. To Make the Sunday School Aggressively Missionary

Chapter 7

Getting the Work Done

IN THE PRECEDING CHAPTER it was set out that the business of the superintendent is to make the Sunday school build the church, to keep the Sunday school growing, to see that the Bible is taught, to make the Sunday school positively evangelistic, to make the Sunday school doctrinally sound, and to make the Sunday school aggressively missionary. In getting the work of a Sunday school done, there are essential methods that a superintendent should use and lead the school to use. Right methods if intelligently and vigorously used will aid in getting the work of a Sunday school done and will produce the maximum results.

If the superintendent stands for progress and for the use of right methods in the Sunday school, he will have the confidence of the officers and teachers, and there will be the note of hopefulness and the spirit of victory in every phase of the work.

I. KEEPING THE SUNDAY SCHOOL PROPERLY ORGANIZED

1. *Enlisting the Necessary General Officers*

The general superintendent should associate with himself the necessary general officers. There should be one or more associate superintendents, and a general secretary.

One associate superintendent may act as general classification officer and see that all new pupils are properly classified and that all visitors are cordially received and cared for. Another associate superintendent may be placed in charge of the enlargement of the school and direct the visitation. There may be an associate superintendent in charge of the training program for the officers and teachers and other workers. The number of associate superintendents needed will depend upon the time the general superintendent can give to the work, upon the size of the Sunday school, the type of building, the available workers, and other things.

A capable, co-operative, cheerful individual should be selected as general secretary. The general superintendent should see that the secretary understands his or her duties, then he should encourage and guide this officer in the important work of gathering an accurate record of each individual and class each week. If the school is departmentized this will be done through the department secretaries. The general secretary is responsible for seeing that each department and class secretary is trained to secure, compile, and interpret the records. The general secretary should also be responsible for ordering, receiving, and distributing the literature each quarter.

The superintendent is also responsible for the organization in every department and class in the Sunday school.

2. *Keeping the Present Organization Intact*

It will require constant effort to keep the present organization intact. If for any reason a vacancy occurs, the superintendent is the one to see that it is filled immediately. It will be well for him to have a list of prospective officers and teachers and see that they take advantage of every training opportunity offered. He can help them by using them as substitute workers, by enlisting them in the training schools, and by seeing that they attend the associational meetings for Sunday school workers. If these things are done, there will be capable workers available for all vacancies.

3. *Enlarging the Organization*

From time to time additional classes should be started and led to succeed. Often it will be necessary to build a new class out of prospects. The present classes should be studied and as often as necessary additional classes organized to take care of crowded conditions and growing situations. Plans should be made in advance of Promotion Day for as many additional classes as will be needed to hold the present enrolment and to make possible a continued increase.

4. Setting Up Departments

It is difficult to build a Sunday school beyond a membership of two or three hundred on the class basis. There are thousands of Sunday schools located even in the open country with a constituency large enough to necessitate departments. If the possibilities require it, the superintendent should set up a department organization for each department as soon as the necessary space can be secured.

5. Seeing That the Classes Are Functioning

As the work of a Sunday school is done in and through the classes, the superintendent should give constant attention to the organization, equipment, and work of the classes. This will include seeing that the classes are properly organized, that they have the necessary equipment and supplies, and that the class officers are trained for their work.

II. DIRECTING THE PROMOTIONAL ACTIVITIES

1. Regular Visitation

Upon the superintendent falls the responsibility of getting regular visitation done in every class in the Sunday school. He should keep the classes supplied with the names of the people who should be in Sunday school and see that the officers and teachers visit every person enrolled and every available prospect. It is the duty of the superintendent to train, inspirit, and lead the officers and teachers in a continuous program of personal visitation.

It is his task to show the need for visitation. People who need the Sunday school most do not attend voluntarily; they must be brought. The superintendent should keep this truth before the officers and teachers. Wherever there are *going* Sunday school officers and teachers, there will be *coming* Sunday school pupils. Continuous growth depends upon regular visitation by the officers and teachers. It is the work of the superintendent to keep before the officers and teachers the New Testament method of visitation. "And daily in the temple, and in every house, they ceased not to teach and preach Jesus Christ" (Acts 5: 42). Not occasionally, as duty demands or custom suggests, but *daily*, as the love of Christ in the heart impels, as the condition of a lost soul compels, as the privilege to serve the Lord and Saviour gives courage of soul and swiftness of hands and feet should the visiting be done. Unless the superintendent keeps the officers and teachers visiting regularly, he will fail in the larger opportunity, no matter what else he may do. It is his duty to adopt definite plans and lead the officers and teachers in regular visitation.

There are many ways and means of getting visiting done. No one way will meet the needs in all churches. There are five things which the general superintendent can do to promote and to secure the highest type of visitation: set the example, have a definite time, make assignments, secure reports, and train the workers. These methods are discussed fully in chapter 2.

2. *Adequate Equipment*

It is the responsibility of the superintendent to provide the officers, teachers, and pupils with the best equipment obtainable. Anything that will enable the officers and teachers to do better work should if possible be secured. The superintendent should see that every class and department in the school has the necessary equipment. It will be necessary for him to hold personal conferences from time to time with each officer and teacher and find out his needs and then lead the church to supply these needs. In the weekly meeting of the officers and teachers the need of each department and of each class should be presented so that all of the officers and teachers understand the needs of the whole school.

In the past, many schools have had to meet in one-room buildings and have all their classes in the church auditorium. As such schools move up to the department pattern, they are providing separate classrooms and assembly rooms, and so increasing their enrolment and the effectiveness of their ministry.

GETTING THE WORK DONE   97

When all of the classes must meet in the same room, the corners should be reserved for the smaller children. If this is done, small chairs can be provided, and the walls can be used for a few good pictures and other necessary material.

It is the task of the superintendent to lead the church to see the need for additional room and then with the pastor lead the church to provide the room. The majority of churches that are now meeting in one-room buildings could provide ample room for the Sunday school and Baptist Training Union if they realized the need. Before any additional rooms are provided, the pastor and superintendent should consult with the state Sunday school secretary or the Department of Church Architecture, Baptist Sunday School Board and be sure that the additional space is properly adapted to the needs of the Sunday school and Baptist Training Union work.

3. Accurate Records

(1) Accurate records are important

The importance of accurate and adequate Sunday school records cannot be overestimated. Their importance in guiding each individual pupil in his work and habits is beyond human calculation. Accurate records will enable Sunday school officers and teachers to place every effort where it seems to be most needed. A Sunday school superintendent who neglects the Sunday school records is failing at a vital point. Suppose a banker should neglect to keep accurate records, or suppose a captain of a ship should fail to keep an account of the position and direction of his ship.

(2) The Six Point Record System is an effective tool

The Six Point Record System is used generally by Southern Baptist Sunday schools. The basis of the system is simple, includes the following six points, and can be used in any Sunday school:

Attendance	Offering
On time	Prepared lesson
Bible brought	Preaching attendance

a. Some values of the Six Point Record System.—The Six Point Record System is first of all a program of work for each individual. Its purpose is to guide the individual in his work, help him build these six habits into his life, and to furnish an incentive for him to do regularly these six things.

The Six Point Record System is also an effective Sunday school method which the officers and teachers can use in their efforts to guide the individual and to know what the individual is doing and what he is not doing.

The Six Point Record System is a Sunday school builder in that it encourages the pupil to come every Sunday. It also places responsibility upon the officers and teachers to see that the pupil does attend regularly and promptly.

The Six Point Record System is an aid to Bible teaching as it encourages the regular study of the lesson and the bringing of the Bible to Sunday school every Sunday.

The Six Point Record System recognizes the principle of systematic giving. The purpose of this point is to train the individual to give regularly.

The Six Point Record System builds the preaching attendance. It provides a strong incentive for each individual to attend the preaching service every Sunday and sets all of the officers and teachers to work at the task of securing the attendance of each individual upon the preaching service.

The Six Point Record System takes the work of a Sunday school out of the field of generalization and personalizes it. It magnifies the individual, locates his needs, and records his progress. It is the business of the general superintendent to see that the Six Point Record System is used, always, to help the individual.

b. Material needed for a class Sunday school—

Form 10. Classification Slip
Form 20. Enrolment Card

Form 30Q. Class or Group Record Card
Form 35Q. Class Record Card
Form 45L. Class Report Envelope
Form   5. Information Card on Six Point Credits
Form 15. Individual Report Envelope
Form 135. Monthly Sunday School Report to Church
Form 125. Monthly Class Report to School or Department
Form 720. School Six Point Record Chalkboard
Form 165. Individual Report Envelope for Extension Department
Form 170. Monthly Extension Group Report
Form 175. Monthly Extension Department Report
Form 180. Monthly Cradle Roll Group Report
Form 155. Monthly Cradle Roll Department Report
School Triplicate Report Book No. 38
Cradle Roll Department Record Book No. 11
Cradle Roll Group Record Book No. 12
Nursery Group Record Book No. 22
Beginner Class Record Book No. 32
Primary Class Record Book No. 42
Junior Class Record Book No. 52
Intermediate Class Record Book No. 62
Young People's Class Record Book No. 72
Adult Class Record Book No. 82
Extension Department Record Book No. 91
Extension Group Record Book No. 92

The enrolment cards, the class cards, and the general secretary's reports are the property of the school and should be kept in the church building, available for the use of the pastor, general superintendent, or other officers. The teacher's book is his property and should remain in his possession.

c. *Installing the record system.*—In the initial installation, every member of the school, including the officers and teachers, should be classified on a designated Sunday morning. The plan and purpose of the record system should be fully explained. Teachers and class officers should see that a classification slip is filled out for every member present. The slips for absentees should be secured promptly. During the week, the information should be transferred to the enrolment cards, class cards, officers' cards and teacher's books.

No name should ever be taken off an enrolment card, class card, or teacher's book or left off when a new list is made, except by agreement of the pastor, general superintendent, general secretary, and teacher of the class.

d. Operating the record system.—New pupils should be classified on the first Sunday they attend. Every blank on the classification slip should be filled in. The classification slip should be filled out in duplicate so that the general secretary and teacher may each have a copy. In department schools it is filled out in triplicate.

The Individual Report Envelope, Form 15, is filled out by each person above Primary age who is present on Sunday. Nursery children are graded only on attendance; Beginners on two points—present and on time. Primary pupils are graded on four points—present, on time, offering, and memory verse. All others are graded on the six points. Records for children under Junior age are marked by teachers, based on observation. Pupils mark their grades under the direction of the teacher in the Intermediate, and Junior groups. The teacher, the class president, and the class secretary should co-operate in securing the records in the classes for Young People and Adults. The class cards should be checked by the teacher or the class officers and turned over to the secretary. If there are no departments the general secretary should fill out the general secretary's card and show the record of the school by classes. In this way, an accurate record can be secured of each individual and each class in the Sunday school.

e. Wrong practices.—The practice of dropping names from the class rolls is wrong, unscriptural, and deadening to the spirit and compassion of the Sunday school workers. There is no reason for dropping a name from the Sunday school roll. If a person dies or moves, his name is automatically taken off the roll, but there is no good reason for dropping the names of pupils if they are prospects for the Sunday school. There are many excuses made, and some of these may sound rather plausible. One excuse is that the irregular pupils lower the record. The purpose of the record is not to have a 100 per cent class, but to keep a complete record of each individual and to guide him in his habits. The lower the individual's percentage, the harder the Sunday school teachers and officers ought to work. Winning each individual to Christ and then putting forth earnest effort to help him grow in grace is better than dropping his name.

It is not right to place all of the responsibility for regular attendance upon the pupil. The officers and teachers should accept the major share of this responsibility. Sunday school officers and teachers who practice the unscriptural habit of dropping names assume a fearful responsibility. Many times those whose names are dropped from the rolls are the lost members of the class. The churches have let the Sunday schools drop from the rolls the names of many thousands of boys and girls and young men and young women between the ages of nine and twenty and thus have lost a vital contact with these young lives.

In some schools on Promotion Day many individuals are promoted into classes that are already full because new classes have not been formed. Because there is no proper provision for the ones promoted, they begin to be irregular. Finally their names are dropped and, alas, many of them never come back. Let the everlasting purpose and the continuous effort be to win the individual to Christ and to whole-hearted Christian service.

Sunday schools should not start new rolls either monthly, quarterly, or annually. To do so breaks vital contact with those not present the day the new roll is made. When new class cards are made, every name, regardless of the number of absences, should be transferred to the new card.

f. Using the record system.—From the Junior classes through the Adults, the records for the day can be displayed at the close of the lesson and used as a basis for encouraging preaching attendance, as well as the improvement of the other five points. The general secretary should see that the record for the school is displayed at some prominent place in the building.

The pastor and general superintendent should co-operate

in presenting the report at the eleven o'clock hour. The pastor can use the report at this time as a basis for helpful suggestions and for honest commendation.

The teacher should keep in the teacher's class book an accurate record of each individual enrolled and should use the record as a guide in leading each individual to do regularly all of the six things outlined.

A careful study should be made of the records in the weekly meeting of the officers and teachers.

Between the last Sunday of one month and the first Sunday of the next month the monthly report cards should be carefully made out and delivered to each pupil in person by the officers and teachers. The best time to do this is on a regular visitation day, and delivering the monthly report card will give a point of contact for each visit. The monthly report card should be used throughout the school.

The pastor, superintendent, teacher, and class officers should each week study the records and plan to make the largest and widest possible use of them.

4. *Weekly Officers and Teachers' Meeting*

This meeting may be held preferably one hour and thirty minutes before the midweek prayer meeting. If the church does not have a regular prayer meeting, the weekly officers and teachers' meeting should be held at the most convenient time.

The weekly officers and teachers' meeting can be made one of the most vital and far-reaching weekday meetings of a church.

The general superintendent must do much of the work through the officers and teachers. It is his task to see that the Sunday school has an adequate number of the right kind of officers and teachers and then to guide them in the work and see that they do the work assigned by the church.

A weekly meeting of the officers and teachers is essential for the proper administration of a Sunday school. Every Sunday school, regardless of location or size, will find a weekly meeting of the officers and teachers highly profitable.

(1) *Every church should have a weekly officers and teachers' meeting*

There are at least six good and sufficient reasons why every Sunday school should have a weekly meeting of the officers and teachers.

a. Because of the possibilities of the Sunday school.—The Sunday school organization provides a group of volunteer workers, capable and susceptible of growing in grace and knowledge, flexible enough for co-operation, and Christian enough to work in the program of a church if informed and led. The Sunday school organization is adjusted so that responsibility is fixed for each age group and for each individual in each age group. The Sunday school is a church's best known opportunity for reaching the masses for regular Bible study. The Sunday school is the only church agency set to teach the Bible to lost people. The Sunday school, because it reaches large numbers of people who are not church members and holds them year after year, makes possible, no doubt, a church's greatest evangelistic opportunity. Tests show that church members who attend Sunday school regularly are far more active in preaching attendance, regular giving, and personal soul-winning than the church members who do not attend Sunday school.

If, therefore, the Sunday school provides a church with its greatest opportunity to reach the masses for regular Bible study, and if the Sunday school provides a church with its greatest evangelistic opportunity, and if the church members who attend the Sunday school give and serve more liberally and more effectively than the church members who do not attend, then surely the possibilities of the Sunday school demand and merit a weekly meeting of the officers and teachers.

And if all this is true, then the weekly meeting of the officers and teachers provides a church with one of its greatest opportunities for encouraging, indoctrinating, and directing the workers who man the organization that gives the church its greatest Bible-teaching, soul-winning, and enlistment opportunity.

b. To see that the Bible is used in every class in the Sunday school.—The temptation of many Sunday school teachers is to follow lines of least resistance and to discuss whatever subject is most familiar to them, regardless of the Scripture assigned or the needs of the individuals of the class. If all the Sunday school teachers attend a weekly meeting and regularly take part in the development and preparation of the lesson, it will help to correct this weakness. It is the business of the superintendent to see that the Bible is used by every teacher in the Sunday school.

c. To study the best methods of presenting the lesson.—A weekly meeting of the officers and teachers provides an opportunity for the mutual study of the Bible in general and the next Sunday's lesson in particular. A weekly meeting of the officers and teachers provides regular opportunities to improve the teaching in content, methods, and spirit.

d. To guarantee unity of purpose and effort.—In a weekly officers and teachers' meeting the superintendent can enlist all of the Sunday school forces in the accomplishment of any and every task the Sunday school should do. This is not possible without frequent meetings of the officers and teachers.

e. To train and inspirit the officers and teachers.—The superintendent can use the weekly officers and teachers' meeting to deepen a sense of responsibility; to develop habits of dependability, faithfulness, punctuality, loyalty, and preparation; to train in the work of personal visitation and personal soul-winning. Sunday school officers and teachers are human beings with human frailties. It is the business of the Sunday school superintendent to encourage and inspirit the officers and teachers and to keep them happy in their work. People are drawn, not driven, into Christian work. The attitude, spirit, and example of the general superintendent will in a large measure mold and shape the attitude, spirit, and work of the officers and teachers. If the superintendent believes in the work of the Sunday school, the officers and teachers will soon come to be more zealous.

The superintendent should stay alone with the Lord until he has decided just how important the work is. He should talk with the pastor about the plans for the Sunday school until some definite decisions have been reached. Then he should come before the officers and teachers once each week with the spirit of the Lord in his heart, the light of heaven in his face, the right conception of the work in his mind, with definite plans to present, with a determined will to give his best, and with a constant plea of love in his voice. Then he will draw the officers and teachers by the force and power of his own earnestness, zeal, example, and happiness. A busy, positive, definite, happy superintendent will attract and inspirit the officers and teachers. It is the duty of the superintendent to create and maintain a winning morale.

f. To make definite plans for the promotion of the work of the Sunday school.—Such matters as visitation, preaching attendance, winning the lost, and Sunday morning programs will need regular attention. Then special efforts, such as training schools, denominational days, promotion time, special occasions, the associational meetings, and many other spiritual matters will need attention.

g. To give constant attention to the spiritual lives of the officers and teachers.—The officers and teachers should pray together for each other and for their pupils. If there were no other reasons for the weekly meeting of the officers and teachers, the spiritual growth and the spiritual quickening of the officers and teachers is sufficient reason for such a meeting. The superintendent should use the weekly meeting to deepen and enlarge the spiritual conception of the officers and teachers and to create and sustain a passion for the lost.

All of these matters should receive constant attention in every Sunday school, no matter what size or where located.

(2) *The class school can schedule a weekly officers and teachers' meeting*

7:00 DEVOTION

Song, prayer, and Scripture reading

7:05 TEACHING IMPROVEMENT PERIOD

This period provides a place for regular study. A study of the lesson, the pupil, methods of teaching, the spiritual needs of the officers, teachers, and pupils, soul-winning, worship, growth, service, giving, and other phases of the work of the Sunday school should receive careful emphasis. The needs are many, and the weekly meeting of the officers and teachers offers a continued opportunity for study and improvement of every phase of the work in the Sunday school. A study of the lesson, and means of improving the quality of Bible-teaching, and methods of enlisting people in Bible study should receive the major emphasis in this period. Suggestions and helps are carried in *The Sunday School Builder* each month. Free literature on the subjects mentioned here can be had by writing to your state Sunday school secretary or to the Baptist Sunday School Board.

7:45 CONFERENCE

The conference period provides an opportunity for a review and study of the reports, for the establishment of aims, in planning for attendance, etc. This conference affords the superintendent and pastor an opportunity to present definite objectives and plans to the officers and teachers. It also provides an opportunity for the superintendent and pastor to speak words of encouragement and commendation.

8:15 PRAYER

If a regular prayer meeting is held, the officers and teachers' meeting would be merged into the prayer service. Otherwise, there should be a definite period for prayer. The pastor, when present, may lead this period; at other times it should be led by the superintendent. Special requests for prayer may be made by those present. Certainly, the lost pupils in the different classes would be a heavy burden on the hearts of the teachers. Likewise, the sick and needy and those in sorrow and trouble of whatever nature would be remembered. Then surely the needs of the teachers and officers themselves would be remembered in this season of prayer.

5. *Training of the Officers and Teachers*

The superintendent should plan for and conduct from one to four training schools each year. One or more of these may be in co-operation with an association-wide effort.

In addition to leading the present corps of officers and

teachers in a training program, the superintendent should select and enlist prospective officers and teachers in all the training classes. He should enlist the capable young people in the training work. He should lead the teachers of the Young People's and Adult classes to co-operate with him in the selection of prospective workers and in leading the prospective workers to attend the training classes.

The superintendent should familiarize himself with the whole of the Sunday school training program and be able to plan the training schools so as to meet the needs of the officers and teachers and through them build the Sunday school and meet the needs of all those enrolled in the Sunday school in the most effective way.

SUGGESTED PROGRAMS FOR WEEK OF TRAINING

Schedule of work—Monday through Friday

7:00 Classwork

7:45 Address or conference on the practical phases of the work in the Sunday school.

8:30 Classwork

9:15 Adjournment

In addition to the regular training schools the officers and teachers should be encouraged to study the books individually.

6. *The Standard of Excellence*

Out of fifty years' experience of pastors, superintendents, and Sunday school workers in general, Southern Baptists have brought together the essential things that every Sunday school should do and have written them down in what is known as the Standard of Excellence. Each of the ten suggestions is essential in the work of a Sunday school. Not one of them can be left out and the work of a Sunday school be well balanced and complete.

The Standard of Excellence is a well-balanced program of work for a Sunday school. Wherever churches have used rightly the Standard of Excellence and the leaders have earnestly tried to see that the ten things suggested have been done, progress has been the result—progress in enlargement, in better Bible teaching, in evangelism, and in giving.

The church should adopt the Standard of Excellence as a program of work for the Sunday school. This action makes it the program of the church and puts the church in charge of the Sunday school. The pastor and the superintendent should offer such a recommendation to the church and request the church to take such action.

When adopted by the church in conference as the program of the Sunday school, the Standard of Excellence at once becomes the superintendent's program. He is then obligated to see that the Sunday school does the things suggested in the Standard of Excellence. The church has spoken, and as a good and faithful church officer the superintendent must act. It also puts the church back of the superintendent in his efforts. It will make it much easier to secure additional workers. It will put the church back of the training program of the Sunday school. It will give the superintendent an opportunity to make frequent reports to the church and thus keep before the church the work of the Sunday school. It also takes the work of the Sunday school out of the field of vagueness and aimlessness and makes the work definite and purposeful.

A constant use of the Standard of Excellence will prevent a Sunday school from getting in a rut. The Standard of Excellence protects and guides a superintendent just as the scale protects and guides a musician.

Any Sunday school anywhere can reach and maintain all of the ten points of excellence in the Standard. In fact the requirements do not deal with equipment, but with the essential things that all Sunday schools should emphasize. A Sunday school with six classes and with a one-room building in which to work can maintain all of the suggestions all of the time. In fact, it may be easier for a small Sunday school to maintain the suggestions than for the larger Sunday schools. However, it is important for any Sunday school to use the Standard of Excellence as a program of work.

7. *Annual Vacation Bible School*

The Vacation Bible school work is now a part of the Sunday school. This makes the superintendent responsible for the promotion of this phase of the Sunday school work. At the beginning of the church year the superintendent should recommend to the church the date when the Vacation Bible school can best be held and ask the church to approve the date. He should then secure the workers, advertise the school, and make all necessary arrangements for the successful promotion of the work.

III. PREPARING AND DIRECTING THE SUNDAY MORNING WORK

1. *The Sunday Morning Programs*

The assembly program will consume at least twenty minutes. If proper preparation has been made, this period will be a time of worship, fellowship, preparation and inspiration. Here is a place to create a demand for each pupil to have his own Bible, bring it to the Sunday school, and use it. The superintendent should be so familiar with his written program that he can go from one part to the next without any hesitancy. All those assigned parts should be in their places so that no time will be lost. Five or ten minutes of this period should be used for the promotional work of the Sunday school. The opportunity afforded for encouraging regular and prompt attendance, urging regular visitation, recognizing good work on the part of classes, teachers, and individuals should be used with care and enthusiasm by the general superintendent.

(1) *The superintendent is responsible for the assembly programs*

The general superintendent is responsible for the assembly program unless the school is departmentized. A good superintendent will not evade this responsibility by asking different classes or groups to assume control. As a rule, such a procedure will mean time taken from the class period, as few classes will stay within the time allotted. It will invariably mean a wrong emphasis. Irrelevant material, no matter how interesting, detracts from the purpose of the Sunday school, gets the minds of the teachers and pupils away from the lesson, and hinders rather than helps. Again, when a class puts on the program, it virtually means no Bible study, for in most instances the time of the teacher has been taken in an effort to assist the class in the preparation of the program. The general superintendent should see that the right kind of program is prepared and presented; and then protect the people from anything that would detract from the purpose of the Sunday school, no matter how interesting it might be.

(2) *The purpose of the program is worship*

The primary purpose of the assembly program is to send the pupils to their classes keen and eager for Bible study and at the same time prepare the teachers in mind and in heart for the important work of guiding the pupils in Bible study. This means that every song, prayer, Scripture reading, and all else done in this time should bear upon the lesson for the day and should create a spirit of reverence and worship. The worship period in a Sunday school is not the place for different individuals or organizations to advertise, make announcements, or promote special interest. It is a time and place for preparation for Bible study, and only those things which will tend to make conditions ideal for Bible study and will lead people to participate in Bible study should be permitted to enter into the worship period.

(3) *The program must be prepared*

The general superintendent should spend as much time and prayer in preparation of the assembly program as he expects the teachers to spend in preparing for their tasks. In fact, the highest success of the teacher's work depends in a large measure upon the kind of program prepared and presented just before the classes assemble for Bible study. The superintendent who waits until he reaches the church building on Sunday morning to select the songs and assign the parts for the worship program is not worthy of his high office.

(4) Secure and use the right materials

The first and most important source of material for the worship program is the Bible. The superintendent should select from the lesson for the day the truth around which he desires to build the program. Next he should search the Bible for related passages, illustrations, stories, and all other material helpful in presenting this truth. Every Sunday school superintendent should receive regularly *The Sunday School Builder*. A suggested program for each Sunday is offered in this magazine and much helpful, rich material is available therein. The superintendent should have the helps available for the teachers, and he should also have additional helps. He should by all means draw his illustrations and materials from different sources from those used by the teachers. The superintendent should have a copy of the songbook used in his church and study it, selecting songs related to the truth around which the lesson centers. The songs are a part of the teaching for the day and should be selected by the superintendent. The Bible, *The Sunday School Builder*, the lesson helps and the songbook will enable the superintendent to build a good program.

2. *The Sunday Morning Schedule*

(1) *The period before the Sunday school opens is vital*

The superintendent should be in the church building at least fifteen minutes before the time for the Sunday school to open. He should see that the building is properly heated and ventilated, that all the equipment is in place, and that all supplies are ready. He need not do all of these things himself, but he should see that they are done. He should see that the officers and teachers are trained to arrive early. He should greet the people as they come and have just the right word for each officer and teacher and for as many of the people as he can meet personally. A proper use of the period before the Sunday school opens will prepare the way for the Sunday school session.

(2) *The period of opening assembly must be well timed*

The superintendent should form the habit of beginning on time and should train the officers, teachers, and pupils to be in their places on time. This part of the program will consume from fifteen to twenty minutes, and the superintendent should see that the program is kept within the time allotted.

(3) *The lesson period must be safeguarded*

Thirty-five to forty minutes should be used for this period. Five to ten minutes of the time should be allowed for securing the reports, and at least thirty minutes of the time for the study of the lesson. The superintendent should see that this period is protected and that the classes get all the time allotted. He should also see that the class officers understand how to co-operate with the teachers in seeing that the thirty minutes assigned for Bible study is not used for any other purpose.

(4) *The closing period merges into the worship service*

In many of the Sunday schools organized on the class basis, there is preaching one Sunday each month. The closing program of the Sunday school should be made on these days to merge into the worship service: A song, a review of the record for last Sunday, and an adequate presentation of the record for the day; recognition of meritorious work of classes, individuals, and teachers; necessary announcements, another song, merging at once without an intermission into the usual worship service. However, on the other three Sundays in the month, there will be more time and a different program can and should be prepared. Twenty to thirty minutes can be used with great profit on the Sundays the church does not have preaching.

QUESTIONS FOR REVIEW

1. What is necessary for the superintendent to keep the Sunday school properly organized?
2. Name seven things the superintendent should do in promoting the work of the Sunday school.
3. Discuss the Sunday morning program.

OUTLINE

I. KEEPING THE SUNDAY SCHOOL PROPERLY ORGANIZED
    1. Enlisting the Necessary General Officers
    2. Keeping the Present Organization Intact
    3. Enlarging the Organization
    4. Setting Up Departments
    5. Seeing That the Classes Are Functioning

II. DIRECTING THE PROMOTIONAL ACTIVITIES
    1. Regular Visitation
    2. Adequate Equipment
    3. Accurate Records
    4. Weekly Officers and Teachers' Meeting
    5. Training of the Officers and Teachers
    6. The Standard of Excellence
    7. Annual Vacation Bible School

III. PREPARING AND DIRECTING THE SUNDAY MORNING WORK
    1. The Sunday Morning Programs
    2. The Sunday Morning Schedule

Chapter 8

The Class Organized and Equipped for Work

THE CLASS is the working unit in a Sunday school. The real work in any Sunday school is done through the classes. One of the major duties of all the administrative officers is to make conditions favorable for the work of the classes. If this is approximated, intelligent and constant attention will have to be given to the classes, all of the classes.

Because the work of the Sunday school is done through the classes, the pastor and general superintendent should give constant and intelligent attention to all of the classes. They should see that there are enough classes, that the classes are thoroughly graded, adequately organized, properly equipped, well housed, and provided with good teachers. They should also see that all of the classes do the work assigned to them by the church.

A Sunday school is not a machine with the classes making up the different mechanical parts. A Sunday school class is made up of human personalities, and each class and each individual will require loving, personal attention.

It is the purpose of this chapter to deal as adequately as space will permit with the work of the classes in the different age groups.

I. AGE GROUPS

1. The Purpose of the Sunday School Determines the Basis of Grading

A Sunday school exists for the purpose of helping to meet the spiritual needs of individuals. Therefore, each individual should be placed in a Sunday school so as to secure the greatest spiritual benefit. This placing of the individual is

114

called grading. The Bible is a wonderful book in that it contains milk for the babes and meat for the strong. The purpose of grading is to make it easier to minister to the spiritual needs of the individual—that is, to give the babes milk and the strong meat. This conception should be the determining factor as to the basis of grading, the size of the classes, and the type of building and equipment. As the spiritual needs of individuals of like ages are more nearly the same, age has been found to be the most effective basis of grading a Sunday school.

2. *The Sunday School and Secular School Differentiated*

The terms "school," "grading," "curriculum," "educational institution," etc., do not necessarily mean that the Sunday school and the secular school have the same purpose or use the same methods. In fact, the aims of the two schools are different. The Sunday school has a positive and distinct purpose—to teach lost people the way of eternal life and to teach saved people to do all the things taught in the Word of God.

Mr. Arthur Flake stated six differences in the Sunday school and the secular school—

> Different constituency
> Different textbooks
> Different basis for grading
> Different methods of building and maintaining
> Different objectives
> Different standards for teachers

While the Sunday school can and, no doubt, should learn many valuable things from the secular school, yet the Sunday school does not aspire to compete with or pattern after the secular school's methods and aims. The Sunday school will find its largest usefulness by holding to the purpose of the Sunday school, and by using the methods best suited for carrying out that purpose. The Sunday school will fulfil its purpose more effectively and more fully by keeping in mind the differences as well as the similarities of the Sunday school and the secular school.

3. *The Age Groups in All Sunday Schools*

There are seven different age groups in every Sunday school. They are grouped in nine classifications:

Cradle Roll—Birth through three years who do not attend
Nursery—Birth through three years who do attend
Beginners—Four and five years
Primaries—Six, seven, and eight years
Juniors—Nine, ten, eleven, and twelve years
Intermediates—Thirteen, fourteen, fifteen, and sixteen years
Young People—Seventeen through twenty-four years
Adults—Twenty-five years and up
Extension—All above four years of age who cannot attend

Two departments, the Cradle Roll and the Extension, are cared for through a home ministry. The rest attend on Sunday morning.

4. *The Three Essential Methods of Keeping the Sunday School Graded*

It is an easy and simple task to keep a Sunday school graded with each individual in the proper place if the leaders will faithfully and regularly do three things. First, classify each individual the first Sunday he comes to Sunday school. Encourage him to enrol immediately. Second, keep adequate records. The Six Point Record System properly installed and intelligently operated will make it possible for the officers and teachers to know at all times just where each individual is classified in the Sunday school. Third, observe annual promotion the last Sunday in September. On this day pupils should be promoted according to their age.

II. ORGANIZATION FOR THE AGE GROUPS

1. *The Cradle Roll Department*

The ministry of the Cradle Roll is in the homes. Through regular visitation it reaches the babies who do not attend

Sunday school. Its objectives are summed up in the slogan "A Christian Home for Every Child." It manifests the interest of the church in the home. It seeks to win unsaved parents to Christ, and to enlist saved parents. Its workers encourage the attendance of the child in Sunday school at the earliest age. It also ministers to expectant parents. Every Sunday school should have a Cradle Roll department. This department offers a major opportunity for evangelism.

The number of workers needed will be determined by the number of children to be ministered to. There should be one visitor for every six to eight homes where there are children for the Cradle Roll department. The suggested workers are:

Superintendent
Associate Superintendent
Secretary
Visitors

The superintendent directs all the work. In communities where there are not more than ten children for the Cradle Roll department, she may do all the work.

The associate superintendent, when needed, shares the work with the superintendent.

The secretary keeps the records and makes out the reports, sends out the birthday cards, the invitations, and assists in all the work.

The visitor should make regular visits to the homes of children assigned to him and do everything he can to encourage and inform the parents in the important work of training the little child. If the mother is not a Christian, the visitor will follow up every opportunity to win her to Christ. The visitor should seek to share the sorrows and joys of the home. He should take *Home Life* magazine, the appropriate series from *Messages to Cradle Roll Parents,* and *Living with Children,* and guide parents in the use of these materials.

2. *The Nursery Departments*

Even the smallest church needs at least two Nursery departments for the children under four who are brought to

Sunday school. There should be a superintendent and other needed workers for each department. Even if there are only two or three babies it is better to have at least two workers.

3. *The Beginner Department*

There should be a teacher or worker for each five to seven children in the age group for the Beginners. This will make possible regular visitation, personal attention, and effective work.

4. *The Primary Department*

In any Sunday school Primary children should have a space by themselves and function as a department with at least two workers. If there are more than eight children, there should be a department organization with a superintendent and a teacher for every five to seven children. A small group makes it easier for a teacher to give personal attention to each person and also makes it easier for the teacher to visit the home of each pupil.

5. *The Classes for Juniors*

The first division of Juniors should be according to sex. If there are as many as ten boys and girls of Junior age in a community, there should be two classes, one for girls and one for boys. There should be a class for every six to eight Junior girls and a class for every six to eight Junior boys.

Junior girls and boys are active. They can accept responsibilities and like to do so.

A simple class organization is suggested for classes for Juniors:

> President
> Vice-president
> Secretary

The term of office should be one quarter. Class meetings should be held monthly. The teacher of the class should always be present in the class meeting. Free literature suggesting class names and duties of class officers, can be had by writing to the Sunday School Department, Baptist Sunday School Board, Nashville, Tennessee, or to your state Sunday school secretary.

6. *The Classes for Intermediates*

Separate classes should be provided for boys and girls in the Intermediate age group, thirteen through sixteen. There should be a class for every six to eight persons. There are not one-half enough classes in the majority of Sunday schools for the Intermediates. It is possible to reach and hold the Intermediates if an adequate number of classes are provided and capable understanding teachers placed in charge.

The suggested officers for an Intermediate class are:

President
Vice-president
Secretary
Group Leaders

A helpful leaflet on the work of an Intermediate class can be secured by writing to your state Sunday school secretary, or to the Sunday School Department, Baptist Sunday School Board, Nashville, Tennessee.

7. *The Classes for Young People*

(1) *Formation of classes*

In making the divisions for young people, first divide by sex, then according to marriage, and then by age. There should be a class for every ten to twenty possibilities. There should be at least two classes for married young people, age seventeen through twenty-four; one class for men and one for women.

The division should be:

Young women, seventeen and eighteen
Young women, nineteen through twenty-four
Young men, seventeen and eighteen
Young men, nineteen through twenty-four

Young married women, seventeen through twenty-four
Young married men, seventeen through twenty-four

In smaller schools fewer classes may be sufficient. In larger schools, more classes will be needed.

(2) *Organization of classes*

Each class should be organized with the following officers:

President
Vice-president
Secretary
Group Leaders

There should be a group leader for every four to six possibilities. The group leaders should be capable, active Christians. The group leaders do their work in personal contacts with the members of their groups and should be chosen with this important work in mind. Literature giving the duties of the class officers can be secured by writing to the Sunday School Department, Baptist Sunday School Board, Nashville, Tennessee, or to your state Sunday school secretary.

(3) *Training the class officers*

The pastor and general superintendent should see that the class officers are trained for their work. There should be a conference immediately after they are elected so that the class officers may understand just what they are expected to do. The class officers should be enlisted in all of the training schools. The class officers should attend the associational meeting for Sunday school workers. The pastor and superintendent should see that the class officers have access to *The Sunday School Builder*. The pastor, superintendent, and teacher should see that regular meetings are held for the class officers. The pastor and superintendent should see that the class officers are informed as to the work of the church and should see also that they understand what part of the work they are expected to do.

8. *The Classes for Adults*

(1) *Formation of classes*

As with the Young People, the first division of classes should be according to sex. The second division should be according to age. There should be a class for every ten to twenty-five Adults. If two classes are sufficient, there should be one class for women and one class for men. If more than two classes are necessary, the division should be:

Women, twenty-five to thirty-four
Women, thirty-five up
Men, twenty-five to thirty-four
Men, thirty-five up

Where more than four classes are needed, closer age groups would be necessary.

(2) *Organization of classes*

Each class for Adults should be organized with the following officers with duties as specified:

President—administration and class guidance
Vice-president—Standards, socials, fellowship, publicity
Group leaders—visitation and personal ministry to members and prospects
Secretary—records, reports, supplies, class funds

This simplified organization has developed in response to the trend toward smaller classes for Adults. It is effective with an enrolment of ten to twenty-five. Since the number on each group is limited to about five, the group leader can minister to the individual needs of each member, seeking to develop him in stewardship, fellowship, Christian service, and personal growth. Regular and irregular members should be evenly distributed in the groups and some prospects assigned to each group. This makes possible a persistent, fruitful visitation ministry directed by the president through the group leaders.

The purpose of the organization is first, to develop the members of the class, and second, to distribute the work of the class.

Literature setting forth the duties of the officers in Adult classes can be had by writing to the Sunday School Department, Baptist Sunday School Board, Nashville, Tennessee, or to your state Sunday school secretary.

(3) *Training the class officers*

The pastor and superintendent should see that the class officers understand what they are to do, that they are trained for their work, and that they do the work assigned by the church and only the work assigned by the church.

Immediately after the election of class officers, a conference should be held, so that the work of the class officers may be outlined and understood. The class officers should be led to attend all of the training schools conducted in the church or the association. They should be led to attend the associational meetings for Sunday school workers. The pastor and superintendent should see that the class officers have access to *The Sunday School Builder*. The pastor, superintendent, and teacher should see that regular meetings of the class officers are held by classes. The pastor and superintendent are responsible for what the class officers do or fail to do.

9. *The Extension Department*

The purpose of the Extension department is to minister to those who cannot come to the Sunday school session on Sunday morning. There is a distinct need for an Extension department in every Sunday school. The necessary officers for an Extension department are:

Superintendent
Associate superintendent
Secretary
Visitors

As the work of the visitor is in the homes and places of business of the people, there should be a visitor for each five to ten possibilities for the Extension department. Each visitor should be given a task commensurate with available time for the work and the ability to do the work.

Literature on the work of the Extension department may be secured by writing to the Sunday School Department, Baptist Sunday School Board, Nashville, Tennessee, or to your state Sunday School secretary.

The pastor and superintendent are responsible for the organization and work of the Extension department. The Extension work is just as much a part of the Sunday school as the class for Junior boys. The field of work for the Extension department is just as definite and just as needy as the field for the classes for men and women. The pastor and superintendent should accept the responsibility for the organization and work of the Extension department.

III. ROOMS AND EQUIPMENT

If possible four or more Nursery rooms should be provided for children birth through three.

Separate classroom space should be provided for each class in a Sunday school, if it is at all possible. However, where all or part of the classes must meet in one room, curtains or screens can be used to provide separate rooms for the classes. While such an arrangement is not ideal, yet it makes the work of a class more effective. Because of the small cost, any church can provide curtains and thus have a separate classroom for every class.

If a Sunday school meets in a one-room building, the corners should be used for the Nursery departments, the Beginners, and the Primaries. Suitable equipment should be provided, and the type of work so necessary with the smaller children made at least partially possible.

The officers and teachers who must work in one-room buildings should not become discouraged. They should remember that thousands of Southern Baptist Sunday schools meet in one-room buildings. They should also remember that excellent work can be done under such conditions. They should not be satisfied with the present arrangement but should seek to move up to a department pattern. From the state Sunday school secretary may be received free literature about the work and equipment for each department, as well as counsel about securing or adapting space for an enlarged organization.

IV. LESSON LITERATURE

Uniform Lessons are prepared for the Primary through the Adult age groups. The following monthly magazines carry Uniform Lesson materials:

> *The Sunday School Builder*
> *The Adult Teacher*
> *The Young People's Teacher*
> *Home Life,* a Christian family magazine

The following quarterlies contain Uniform Lesson materials adapted to the specific needs of the age group involved:

> *Sunday School Adults*
> *Sunday School Young Adults*
> *Sunday School Married Young People*
> *Sunday School Young People*
> *Sunday School Intermediate Pupil*
> *Intermediate Teacher*
> *Sunday School Junior Pupil*
> *Junior Teacher*
> *Sunday School Primary Pupil*
> *Primary Teacher*
> *On Wing with the Word* (ungraded)
> *Sunday School Extension Department Quarterly*

In the Graded Lesson series there is a teacher book and a pupil book for each year from six through sixteen.

Beginner lesson materials are group graded. The same course is offered for class and department schools:

> *Beginner Bible Story,* a set of pupil leaflets
> *Beginner Teacher*

In all the lesson courses large teaching pictures are available for the age groups, Nursery through Junior. They are ordered along with the literature.

The material for the correlated church Nursery program, introduced in October, 1957, is used by both Sunday school and Training Union workers.

> *The Church Nursery Guide*, for those who work with the children in the church
>
> *Living with Children*, distributed by Cradle Roll and Nursery workers, for use by parents in the home

V. CLASS STANDARDS

A program of work, known as the class Standard of Excellence, has been prepared for classes Junior through Adult. The Nursery, Beginner, and Primary age groups do not have classes. In their activity programs, they always function as departments, even in the small Sunday school. There is a Standard of Excellence for each department from the Cradle Roll through the Extension, and group Standards for the Cradle Roll departments.

The general superintendent should see that each class has a copy of the appropriate Standard and actively lead the teacher and class officers to use the Standard. The requirements can all be met and maintained by classes that must meet in one-room buildings, if the leaders will take the lead.

Right use of the Standard will enable a class to do well-balanced work, and the maximum amount of work. The class Standard will keep a class rightly related to the church and its work and to the school and its program. Perhaps the most effective means the pastor and superintendent can use in getting all of the classes to do all of the time what they ought to do is to ask the church to adopt the class Standards for the different age groups as programs of work for the different classes. This puts the church back of the work of every class. In this way the church can say definitely just what each class should do. It also makes the work of each class definite. The adoption of all the class Standards by the church unifies the work and puts all of the Sunday school at work doing the same thing.

QUESTIONS FOR REVIEW

1. Name the nine age groups in a Sunday school and give the age limits of each.
2. Name the three essential methods in keeping a Sunday school graded.
3. Give the necessary organization for a Cradle Roll department.
4. Discuss the organizations for classes in the Junior, Intermediate, Young People's, and Adult groups.

OUTLINE

I. AGE GROUPS

    1. The Purpose of the Sunday School Determines the Basis of Grading

    2. The Sunday School and Secular School Differentiated

    3. The Age Groups in All Sunday Schools

    4. The Three Essential Methods of Keeping the Sunday School Graded

II. ORGANIZATION FOR THE AGE GROUPS

    1. The Cradle Roll Department

    2. The Nursery Department

    3. The Beginner Department

    4. The Primary Department

    5. The Classes for Juniors

    6. The Classes for Intermediates

    7. The Classes for Young People

    8. The Classes for Adults

    9. The Extension Department

III. ROOMS AND EQUIPMENT

IV. LESSON LITERATURE

V. CLASS STANDARDS

Chapter 9

The Teacher at Work

I. JESUS THE GREAT TEACHER

"Rabbi, we know that thou art a teacher come from God," says Nicodemus in the third chapter of John. Martha said to Mary, "The Teacher is here and calleth for thee." Jesus, on that last night said to his disciples, "Ye call me, Teacher, and, Lord: and ye say well; for so I am." (John 13: 13 ASV) Jesus is the great, the matchless Teacher. Jesus is the perfect Exemplar for Sunday school teachers. May all those who are called to teach his Word sit daily at his feet and learn of him what to teach and how to teach.

Three qualities of the great Teacher are given for study and emulation.

1. *He Had a Driving Compassion for the Lost and Needy*

"When Jesus saw the multitudes he had compassion upon them." He had compassion upon the multitudes because of what he is. God is love, and Jesus came from the heart of God to reveal God to the world. Jesus cannot help having compassion because of what he is. The closer Sunday school teachers are to Jesus the stronger and deeper will be their compassion for the lost and needy. Quite often Sunday school teachers and those who ought to be teachers excuse their shortcomings and failures with the statement that they do not have time. Mostly it is not a question of time, but of desire. Usually it is not a matter of time but of Christlikeness. "For where your treasure is, there will your heart be also" (Matt. 6:21). The attitude toward the unreached multitudes and the efforts put forth to reach the lost will be in proportion to the Christlike compassion in the heart. Seeking the absentees will be a privilege if the heart is filled with compassion. Winning new pupils will be a joy if the heart is burdened for the lost. Preparing the lesson will never grow old if the salvation of some lost soul is the motive. Attending the weekly officers and teachers' meeting will be looked forward to if the multitudes are constantly on the heart.

The disciples were commanded to tarry in Jerusalem until power came. The weekly officers and teachers' meeting, the prayer meeting, the training schools, the associational Sunday school conferences, regular Bible study, and the private devotional hours should be waiting places where the Sunday school teacher will pray, seek and wait for power.

2. *He Had a Thorough-Going Sincerity in Life and Words*

Sincerity is found in every recorded utterance of Jesus. Jesus was sincere in proclaiming who he was. He was sincere in proclaiming what he came for. The devil tempted him with the power and honor of the world. Jesus replied with the Word of God. He was sincere as he faced the cross. Pilate asked him the question, "Art thou the king of the Jews?" and Jesus answered, "Thou sayest." He was sincere in telling man of his lost condition. Nicodemus was a ruler, educated, cultured, honest, and sincere, yet Jesus told him plainly that he must be born again.

Sunday school teachers are tempted even as Jesus was tempted. They are tempted by the praises of man to bring messages that are pleasing to selfish and sinful ears. They are tempted to appear to know when they do not know. They are tempted to discuss what they think rather than to open the Bible and let the Word speak. Sunday school teachers should be sincere in thought and in life. They should be sincere in what they teach.

3. *He Dealt with People as They Were*

Jesus called Peter, Andrew, James, John, and the others to follow him. He began his ministry with them on their own plane. He invited them to follow him and promised that he would make them to become fishers of men. He asked them to enrol in his school and learn of him. He looked at Simon Peter and saw a potential character, strong and firm as a rock. There were the months and years of changing conceptions and training before Peter measured up to the ideal Jesus set for him.

Jesus made himself the friend of the twelve and won their confidence by sharing their experiences. He lived with them. They lived with him. He walked with them. They walked with him. He talked to them. They talked to him. He asked them questions. They asked him questions. He believed in them. They believed in him. He trusted them. They learned to trust him. He loved them. They learned to love him. He knew their possibilities and their limitations. When teachers have walked with those whom they would teach, when they have known them and loved them and shared their confidence, then lessons will cease to be essays with little or no relation to those who hear them, and will become instead the sharing of experiences from one heart to another.

In all his teaching Jesus drew his illustrations from things familiar to his hearers. He seemed to have their needs, their capacities, and their environment in mind when he taught them. In many Sunday school classes, even of adult men, some of those enrolled do not have Bibles they can call their very own. No doubt much the teacher says is out of the range of knowledge or experience of the majority of those present. The teacher should begin with the individuals where they are and lead on gradually.

Jesus selected the twelve to be with him and to be his pupils. It is not known why he did not select more. No doubt Sunday school workers could profit by a careful study of the methods of Jesus in this connection. Many Sunday school teachers scorn the idea of small classes. Jesus considered it worthy of his time to teach just twelve.

Surely Sunday school teachers would profit by striving to learn and follow these qualities of the great Teacher.

II. The Teacher's Task

1. *The Teacher and the Bible*

The teacher's task is to plant the Word of God in the hearts and minds of each individual in the class. This is just as true in the Nursery as in the class for adult men. In fact, youth is the planting time of life, and workers with children should use all of the precious minutes allotted to the class period to plant the Word of God in the minds and hearts of the pupils. From a babe Timothy knew the Scriptures. Every child has a right to know the Scriptures from babyhood. The Word planted in human hearts by Sunday school teachers has been the means for the salvation of multitudes. There is no more serious business in life than teaching the words of eternal life to dying men. Of course, this will include getting the person to attend, it will include proper equipment, it will include helpful lesson literature, it will include right atmosphere, it will include right schedules, it will include preaching attendance, and much more. However, the task of the Sunday school teacher is to teach the Bible. A leading pastor has said: "We cannot stress too strongly the need of the release of God's Word on the human heart and the dependence upon the Holy Ghost for conviction, regeneration, salvation, and illumination. We ought to stay straight on what we teach—the Bible."

In Matthew 28:19, 20, we have the recorded words of Jesus, "Go ye therefore, and teach all nations, baptizing them in the name of the Father, and of the Son, and of the Holy Ghost: teaching them to observe all things whatsoever I have commanded you: and, lo, I am with you alway, even unto the end of the world. Amen."

Paul in 2 Timothy 2:15 told Timothy to study. However, notice that Paul told Timothy to "study to shew thyself approved unto God, a workman that needeth not to be ashamed, *rightly dividing the word of truth.*"

The Sunday school teacher should heed the admonition of Paul to Timothy and stick to the task of teaching the Bible in the most effective way.

2. *The Teacher and the Individual*

The teacher should strive continuously to do all of the following things for each individual. The teachers of Nursery, Beginner and Primary pupils may not have the joy of actually winning the individual to Christ or of enlisting the individual in service. However, if their work is well done, they are preparing the life for an early definite decision for Christ, and laying the foundation for a life of loving, fruitful service. A good objective for the teacher would be to win each individual—

> To regular attendance
> To regular Bible study
> To regular preaching attendance
> To Christ as Saviour
> To church membership
> To pray without ceasing
> To regular attendance at Training Union
> To some form of definite Christian service
> To regular, systematic giving
> To become a soul-winner

Bible study and regular preaching attendance are conditions under which lost people are led to see themselves sinners in the sight of God and to turn to Christ in repentance and faith for salvation.

Systematic Bible study, earnest prayer, regular preaching attendance, active Christian service, and cheerful, wise giving, are the conditions under which Christian personality develops. It is the business of the teacher to lead the individual to do these things regularly and sincerely. These are the conditions to fulfil in order for lost persons to find Christ and for Christians to grow in grace and in the knowledge of the Lord and Saviour, Jesus Christ.

III. The Teacher's Motive

The Sunday school teacher's motive is set out in the following scriptures: "And he that sent me is with me: the Father hath not left me alone; for I do always those things that please him" (John 8:29). "Jesus saith unto them, My meat is to do the will of him that sent me, and to finish his work" (John 4:34). "And whatsoever we ask, we receive of him, because we keep his commandments, and do those things that are pleasing in his sight" (1 John 3 : 22). A Sunday school teacher will find his greatest joy in doing the will of God.

In 2 Timothy 2 : 15 Paul exhorts Timothy to study to show himself *approved unto God*. If the teacher's motive is to please God, the work will be done to the best of the teacher's ability.

IV. The Teacher's Relationship to the Church

Every teacher, whether in the Nursery or in the class for adult men, should be elected by the church. The teacher is the connecting link between the class and the church. The teacher, as a church officer, becomes responsible to the church for the co-operation of the class with all the work of the church. The pastor and general superintendent represent the church in the selecting, enlisting, and training of the teachers. Their recommendations should be made to the church in conference, and the church should elect the teachers, all of them. Every teacher through the general superintendent should render regularly to the church an account of his stewardship as a church officer. This applies to all Sunday school officers, including the workers in the Cradle Roll and Extension departments.

The teacher has a right to expect every possible help and support from the church. The church, through the pastor and superintendent, should see that each teacher has a good meeting place for the class, all necessary equipment, adequate supplies of literature, etc.

V. The Teacher's Responsibility to the Sunday School

The highest success of a Sunday school demands the co-operation of all the officers and teachers. A Sunday school class is just one unit in the Sunday school. The greatest success of one unit depends upon the success of every other unit or class. The one teaching the nine-year boys should realize that what was done with these same boys while they were eight and what will be done for them when they are ten has much to do with whether his work will count for the most. Thus it is true throughout all of the Sunday school. Every teacher should be interested in the whole life of each individual. The Sunday school exists for the purpose of ministering to the spiritual needs of the individual. Therefore the teacher of the twelve-year boys should be interested in the class for the six-year children. In a few years he will have those who are now six. It is of great importance for the teacher to co-operate in every part of the work of the Sunday school.

1. *To Build the Class*

The attendance of people in Sunday school is voluntary. Therefore, because of the many attractions outside, because of human weaknesses, and because of the sinfulness of sin, the majority of people must be invited repeatedly to come to Sunday school. With Nursery children, Beginners, Primaries, and Juniors the teacher will have to do all of the visiting. With Intermediates, Young People, and Adults the class members can assist in the work of building the class. However, this does not relieve the teacher of his personal responsibility in visiting himself or in getting the class officers to visit. If a person is habitually absent, it is an indication of a spiritual need. The task of the teacher is to minister to the spiritual needs of each person who should be in the class. The method of Jesus was "For the Son of man is come to *seek* and to save that which was lost." The command of Jesus is "go out into the highways and hedges, and compel them to come in."

2. *To Attend the Weekly Officers and Teachers' Meeting*

Every Sunday school should have a weekly officers and teachers' meeting or a monthly meeting, and every teacher should attend. It is necessary for unity of effort throughout the school. It is needed for the highest success of the school. A weekly officers and teachers' meeting, in addition to being a place for promotion, planning, study, fellowship, and prayer, is a place for an exchange of ideas. Those with the greater advantages should come to help those with less experience, and certainly those with less experience should come for help.

3. *To Be Regular and Prompt in Attendance*

The fifteen-minute period before the Sunday school opens should be used by the teacher just as carefully and intelligently as any part of the Sunday school session. The teacher will need this time to greet and learn to know the members of the class. With Juniors, Intermediates, Young People, and Adults, the teacher should watch this period for every opportunity to speak a brief word to lost persons. The teacher should form a habit of regularity and not let less important things interfere with the opportunity to use every teaching opportunity on Sunday morning.

4. *To Use the Six Point Record System*

If the Sunday school uses the Six Point Record System, then each teacher should use it and see that it is used in the class. Sometimes Sunday school workers get the idea that they can co-operate with the Sunday school in its methods or not, just as they like. They can accept the opportunity offered to teach in the Sunday school or reject it. However, when they accept the position as a teacher, they accept the obligation to co-operate with the Sunday school. After the Sunday school adopts a method, it is not an optional matter with teacher or class as to whether the methods should be used in the class. Fairness and loyalty demand that they co-operate.

5. *To Attend the Training Schools Fostered by the Church*

New study is necessary to give freshness and zest to the teaching. The frequent training courses offer opportunities for Sunday school teachers to add to their store of general knowledge and thus better equip themselves for greater service.

The teachers of Young People and Adults should co-operate with the pastor and general superintendent in leading their members to attend the training classes.

VI. The Teacher's Preparation

1. *The Wider Preparation*

In a period of a few years any intelligent man or woman can learn the great Bible truths and also learn where to find them in the Bible. While the majority of Sunday school teachers may not own many books or have access to a good library, yet nearly every one can have a few good books that will help in the study of the Bible, and the preparation for effective teaching.

Eleven definite practical suggestions that will help Sunday school teachers to make their general preparation are given. Practically all of these suggestions are in reach of all Sunday school teachers.

> Form the habit of daily prayer.
>
> Do regularly the daily Sunday school Bible readings.
>
> Prepare carefully every Sunday school lesson.
>
> Read at least one book in the Bible each month, preferably a book related to the lessons for that time.
>
> Attend all training schools featured by the church or association.
>
> Attend the weekly officers and teachers' meeting.
>
> Attend the Baptist Training Union. If the church does not have one, organize one.
>
> Spend at least ten hours each month in personal visitation.
>
> Try to win at least one lost person to Christ each week.
>
> If the church does not have frequent training schools, complete by individual study at least four of the books in the Sunday School Training Course every year.
>
> Attend all of the associational conferences for Sunday school workers.

A regular participation in these eleven simple things will keep a Sunday school teacher growing.

2. *The Specific Preparation*

A good Sunday school teacher will want to make careful,

prayerful, adequate preparation of each lesson. This will require will power, for the flesh is weak and the devil is active. Of course, the teacher should have a good reference Bible and know how to use it. The Sunday school lesson helps prepared for both teacher and pupil are splendid and will guide the busy teacher in a well-rounded study of the lesson in the briefest possible time. Let the teacher keep in mind that he is a teacher, not a lecturer or an entertainer. A teacher is a guide. A teacher is one who inspirits. A teacher is one who finds the truth needed by the one to be taught and then helps the person to see, understand, and desire the truth.

A good reference Bible and the teacher's quarterly will enable a teacher to prepare well for each lesson. If other material can be had, so much the better. If possible, the teacher should begin the preparation of the lesson early in the week. Of course, there should be the most careful preparation late in the week. An Intermediate boy remarked that if the teachers knew more about the lesson, the Sunday school would be much better.

Then there is the personal preparation or the preparation of the teacher himself. If possible, the teacher should be in the best of physical shape. Even more essential is the spiritual preparation of the teacher. Earnest prayer, a sincere desire to please Christ, an impelling passion for the lost are all essential to the best work of a teacher.

VII. The Teacher in the Classroom

The classroom period brings the teacher face to face with perhaps the major opportunity of the week. Every item of detail should be well planned. The equipment, the schedule, the temperature of the room, the supplies, the records should all be cared for. The teacher, and if with Young People and Adults the class officers, should co-operate in seeing that everything is ready for the lesson period.

If the teacher has won the confidence, love, and respect of the pupils, and if the teacher has made adequate preparation, the thirty minutes for the actual lesson period should and will be the high place in the Sunday school program for Sunday morning. The teacher will see that each individual has a Bible. Carefully and prayerfully the teacher will guide and lead in the study of the Word of God for the thirty minutes.

The importance of the work in the classroom merits the most careful preparation of the teacher, the lesson, and the physical conditions. When the lesson period is not a success, usually it is because the teacher has not made the necessary preparation.

Each person in the class needs God. The Bible contains the revelation of God to man. As the teacher prepares for the lesson period, he will be conscious of the pupils' needs and of the Word of God as the only adequate source for meeting these needs. The teacher will also be conscious of the command of God to teach his Word and of his promises to bless his Word. With such preparation, in faith the teacher can face the class confidently, conscious that he is doing the will of God, that he has the blessings of Jesus, and the guiding support of the Holy Spirit.

May the host of faithful teachers in the Sunday schools seek to emulate the qualities and methods of the great Teacher. May they be true to his teachings and to the spirit of his teaching. May they ever be conscious of the condition of a lost soul and of the possibilities of a life. May they be sure of Jesus as the sufficient and only Saviour. May they be diligent in preparation, compassionate in spirit, and upright in life. May they be fully conscious of the importance of their work in winning the lost to Christ and in the building of Christian character.

QUESTIONS FOR REVIEW

1. Name three qualifications of the great Teacher.
2. What is the teacher's task? Give the motive of the teacher.
3. Discuss the teacher's preparation.
4. Discuss the teacher in the classroom.

OUTLINE

I. JESUS THE GREAT TEACHER
1. He Had a Driving Compassion for the Lost and Needy
2. He Had a Thorough-Going Sincerity in Life and Words
3. He Dealt with People as They Were

II. THE TEACHER'S TASK
1. The Teacher and the Bible
2. The Teacher and the Individual

III. THE TEACHER'S MOTIVE

IV. THE TEACHER'S RELATIONSHIP TO THE CHURCH

V. THE TEACHER'S RESPONSIBILITY TO THE SUNDAY SCHOOL
1. To Build the Class
2. To Attend the Weekly Officers and Teachers' Meeting
3. To Be Regular and Prompt in Attendance
4. To Use the Six Point Record System
5. To Attend the Training Schools Fostered by the Church

VI. THE TEACHER'S PREPARATION
1. The Wider Preparation
2. The Specific Preparation

VII. THE TEACHER IN THE CLASSROOM

DIRECTIONS FOR THE TEACHING AND STUDY
OF THIS BOOK FOR CREDIT

I. DIRECTIONS FOR THE TEACHER

1. Ten class periods of forty-five minutes each, or the equivalent, are required for the completion of a book for credit.

2. The teacher should request an award on the book taught.

3. The teacher shall give a written examination covering the subject matter in the textbook. The examination may take the form of assigned work to be done between the class sessions, in the class sessions, or as a final examination.

Exception: All who attend all of the class sessions; who read the book through by the close of the course; and who, in the judgment of the teacher, do the class-work satisfactorily may be exempted from taking the examination.

4. Application for Sunday school awards should be sent to the state Sunday school department on proper application forms. These forms should be made in triplicate. Keep the last copy for the church file, and send the other two copies.

II. DIRECTIONS FOR THE STUDENT *

1. *In Classwork*

(1) The student must attend at least six of the ten forty-five minute class periods to be entitled to take the class examination.

(2) The student must certify that the textbook has been read. (In rare cases where students may find it impracticable to read the book before the completion of the classwork, the teacher may accept a promise to read the book carefully within the next two weeks. This applies only to students who do the written work.)

(3) The student must take a written examination, making a minimum grade of 70 per cent, or qualify according to *Exception* noted above.

2. *In Individual Study by Correspondence*

Those who for any reason wish to study the book without the guidance of a teacher will use one of the following methods:

(1) Write answers to the questions printed in the book, or

(2) Write a summary of each chapter or a development of the chapter outlines.

In either case the student must read the book through.

Students may find profit in studying the text together, but where awards are requested, individual papers are required. Carbon copies or duplicates in any form cannot be accepted.

All written work done by such students on books for Sunday school credit should be sent to the state Sunday school secretary.

III. THIS BOOK GIVES CREDIT IN SECTION II OF THE SUNDAY SCHOOL TRAINING COURSE.

* *The student must be fifteen years of age or older to receive Sunday school credit.*